# Repo

## *The Church in Foreclosure*

John R. Bost

www.xulonpress.com

*I think we ought to read only books that bite and sting us. If the book we are reading doesn't shake us awake like a blow on the skull, why bother reading it in the first place? . . . A book must be the axe for the frozen sea within us.*

Kafka to Oscar Plook, 1904
*Joyful Exiles* by James M. Houston

# Contents

# Foreword

In my experience, prophetic calls to the church come in two ways. The first comes out of the wounds of the prophetic voice, which in the midst of his or her pain sees how the church should be different. Because these perspectives are so deeply rooted in personal perspective and pain they are often tinged with hurt and anger and thus are easily dismissed by those being spoken to whether or not they bear truth from God.

The second kind of prophet comes as a coach-an encourager-a lover of the kingdom of God-who sees in the church a straying from what might be-perhaps the very mandate of God Himself-and longingly calls the church to reclaim what she was created in the mind of God to be. This prophetic message includes the sad results of choices that are comparable to choosing to be infatuated with plastic beads and costume jewelry while an inheritance of gems of great value and heritage lie forgotten, covered with dust in the dark recesses of a forgotten closet. This prophet calls us to discover what is truly valuable and warns that God will not leave us to toy with the fraudulent and unimportant. Attention to this kind of prophetic call ought not be dismissed for it calls us, in love, to re-claim our inheritance as beloved children of the most High God who, if we allow Him to work through us will begin to bring about His kingdom through us.

John Bost is of the second kind of these prophetic voices. He is in love with the Bridegroom whose goal is to present His bride, the church, to Himself spotless and without wrinkle and that she might do His work in this world, preparing for His coming. I have known John for most of the eighteen years I have served as a mainline pastor in the city where both of us live. John has been a faithful part of his own tradition, serving in the church and seeking to be involved in ministry to the city. But John's vision for the work of Christ has gone well beyond his own tradition, seeking to work with disciples of other traditions pairing up in such a way that each can be faithful to their own tradition, yet deeply involved in bringing the distinctive of the Kingdom of God to a whole city.

When Jesus was asked by John the Baptist if He was the messiah, Jesus responds, "The blind receive sight, the lame walk, those who have leprosy are cured, the deaf hear, the dead are raised, and the good news is preached to the poor." John Bost believes that as Jesus was sent into the world, we too are sent in His name into the world—especially to the cities in which we live, to make a measurable difference. As he has worked with churches, he has been distressed that so often churches are so occupied with the 'stuff' of being a local church, that the opportunity of reaching and impacting a city has no energy available for it. It is as if the way we have chosen to do and be the church in modern America has sapped all the energy away from the activities that Jesus identifies as being core to his Kingdom. If that is true, is our Lord willing to sit by while we ignore His calling? Will He 'repossess' His church, calling us to rediscover the incredible wealth of our gifts, for some time now shut away in some dark closet?

Please read the thoughts of this man—a man who loves the church, yet sees her ignoring the important call God has given her—who raises a prophetic word that we just might need to hear!

Rev. Russ H. Ritchel Jr., M.Div., D.Min.

# Preface

On December 28, 2008, according to my journal, this particular book was birthed. That morning I found myself contemplating what my last twenty years of potential service to the Lord might look like. While in prayer, my request became that He provide for me a fresh word of instruction for what likely would be the final leg of my life journey. Ironically, I am sixty years of age, an interesting threshold in time as I finish the third trimester of my life. I have always loved stories, and in these last twenty years, I have tried to journal my own, even capturing an autobiography in a yet unpublished manuscript entitled "Kingdom Business."

*Trimester* is a term with familiar implications among obstetricians, and for this late-term aspiring writer with heart now fully dilated, it became clear that it was time for me to deliver a book! The reality that came to me was that I had spent the first twenty years of my life hearing about God in church and from my faithful parents; then twenty years were spent personally seeking after God through service within various churches; and now twenty years have been exhausted in the application of principles learned in full service to the community.

I have had a wonderful life, and as Jill Carattini of Ravi Zacharias International Ministries offered on May 23, 2007:

> "'Life is too good,'" She quotes from a friend of F. W. Boreham, "'to be allowed, at its conclusion, to pass from sight.'" Carattini then continues: "His dictum was followed by the theory that every person should sit down and write his or her autobiography.... Though perhaps for reasons other than readership or legacy, I do believe, like Boreham's acquaintance, that there is good reason for every man or woman to tell his or her story. To sit down, without the often-misguiding pressure of making our lives a story for reading, and put our lives in ink is an exercise in living. The pivotal passages of life are worth examining through different lenses of time and space. Autobiography is, as someone said, a seismograph of the soul."[1]

Current mortality rates would indicate that I am truly facing the last leg of my journey. Yes, in football language, I am in the red zone, my last twenty yards on the field; and just like that game played with a pigskin, this wineskin of mine could potentially be facing both the most challenging and most rewarding years of its life.

That December morning as I sat in earnest conversation with God, His response to my question about using this last opportunity to score for Him was answered swiftly, as if He had been waiting for me to pose the question. The reply to my spiritual inquiry was *repent, reposition,* and *replenish.*

Those three words sank deep into my soul, both as words of comfort and promise. I took those thoughts to mean that if I would *repent,* probably referencing the baggage accumulated over the last sixty years, He would *reposition* my life for His service and *replenish* both my strength and my resources for the days ahead. Who wouldn't become thrilled at the possibility of such extended impact and renewal?

As would any passionate Christ follower, I began to share those words with my dearest friends, both for accountability and for wise counsel. I focused on opening myself totally to His Word and His will so as to allow patience to have its perfect work in me, affording the true confession, the pure repentance, and the cleansing that Paul recommends for renewing one's desire (2 Cor. 7:11). The thought that God would reposition my life in His kingdom during my own red zone of play was thrilling.

Yet within only a few weeks and during a similar early morning devotional, while my mind was on a completely different trajectory, I heard the words again: *repent, reposition,* and *replenish.* This time, with the words came a sense of instruction to reconsider the words, both for concept and context. Amidst the intensity of the failing economy of 2009, replete with discussions regarding bank bailouts and global crises, I found myself repeating the words, "Repent, reposition, replenish."

I pondered the alliteration still further—*rep*ent, *rep*osition, *rep*lenish—when suddenly I heard a word deep in my spirit, a word now very familiar to those who have suffered the personal grief of repossession of goods and homes through recent foreclosures: *repo*. The United States was gripped by a recession unlike any since the 1930s, its financial and political institutions guilty of enabling unsustainable debt while its pulpits proclaimed prosperity. Into this context came the word *repo*.

Immediately out of my spirit followed a well-known chapter from John's Revelation:

> And one of the elders saith unto me, Weep not: behold, the Lion of the tribe of Judah, the Root of David, hath prevailed to open the book [often translated as a "scroll" or "deed"], and to loose the seven seals thereof.
>
> And I beheld, and, lo, in the midst of the throne and of the four beasts, and in the midst of the elders, stood a Lamb as it had been slain, having seven horns and seven eyes, which are the seven Spirits of God sent forth into all the earth. And he came and took the book [the deed] out of the right hand of him that sat upon the throne. And when he had taken the book, the four beasts and four and twenty elders fell down before the Lamb, having every one of them harps, and golden vials full of odours, which are the prayers of saints. And they sung a new song, saying, Thou art worthy [as a near kinsman] to take the book [deed], and to open the seals thereof: for thou wast slain, and hast redeemed us to God by thy blood out of every kindred, and tongue, and people, and nation; And hast made us unto our God kings and priests: and we shall reign on the earth. And I beheld, and I heard the voice of many

angels round about the throne and the beasts and the elders: and the number of them was ten thousand times ten thousand, and thousands of thousands; Saying with a loud voice, Worthy is the Lamb that was slain to receive power, and riches, and wisdom, and strength, and honour, and glory, and blessing. And every creature which is in heaven, and on the earth, and under the earth, and such as are in the sea, and all that are in them, heard I saying, Blessing, and honour, and glory, and power, be unto him that sitteth upon the throne, and unto the Lamb for ever and ever. And the four beasts said, Amen. And the four and twenty elders fell down and worshipped him that liveth for ever and ever.

—Revelation 5:5–14

Could we be living in the era in which the Lamb repossesses the deed to His church and, in fact, rightfully repositions her in the land, thus bringing to pass the prayers of founders and saints across America? After this rightful repossession would God then restore our land?

This book was never intended as a message of condemnation, but rather a message of hope and comfort for those who truly love the church, the body of Christ, so many of whom sit trapped in the pews of the institutional churches of our day. My hope is that it will serve as a wakeup call to those pastors now far removed from public life, some simply maintaining their sanctuaries or worse yet remaining silent within those sanctuaries as they await Christ's return. But the kingdom of God is already among us and has been since Calvary. Hosanna to the King!

Will He return some day? Absolutely! What will be the circumstances surrounding His return? I am no longer certain.

I recall Dr. Morris Cerullo, a well-known Pentecostal evangelist, stating prophetically in a meeting that took place years ago that nothing ever happens in the physical world that is not preceded by something that happens within the heavenlies. The physical world simply manifests the spiritual. I believe the financial, moral, and social challenges of 2009 first occurred in the spiritual, maybe decades ago as the watchmen of the church withdrew from the real world. As one pastor iterated, "Like children we crawled into our own spiritual tree houses and pulled the rope up behind us." Our churches have become places of entertainment for congregants and their families, while others are trapped in hollow cocoons of religious sanctuaries twice dead. Either way, the church has left behind a secular society, possibly the natural vacuum created when the sacred withdraws.

However, God is in control, and though generations may pass, justice is sure, and mercy is abundant. I trust this to be a book of prophetic promise that if the church will repent, Christ will reposition her on a planet that is now bereft of hope and, in that repositioning, replenish the church's health and thus our land. That is the promise we have from His Word. "If my people, who are called by my name, will humble themselves and pray and seek my face and turn from their wicked ways, then will I hear from heaven and will forgive their sin and will heal their land" (2 Chron.7:14 NIV).

# Acknowledgments

No one gets the last word about one's life, for that word comes only from those with whom that individual has loved and served. If one has not loved, not served, one has not truly lived.

Solomon said, "Two are better than one; because they have a good reward for their labour. For if they fall, the one will lift up his fellow: but woe to him that is alone when he falleth; for he hath not another to help him up. Again, if two lie together, then they have heat: but how can one be warm alone? And if one prevail against him, two shall withstand him; and a threefold cord is not quickly broken" (Eccles. 4:9–12).

My life has been built around many people, but with my wife, my daughter, and my parents, I have experienced the joy and strength of the threefold cord. I have had a marvelous life with them, yet it would have been even more impacting had I truly taken every opportunity to love and know them better. They have always been there for me, even though often neglected by me. You see, leaders do not become leaders alone. Just as warriors of old had their armor bearers, leaders of today have those few without whom they cannot lead. My parents, my wife, and my daughter have been those constants in my life.

My dad has always guarded my dream, partially because it was his own. He cared enough to share what He felt God had spoken to Him about his sons. He was obedient enough to call a busy son at times, not knowing why but willing to deliver just a few words that meant the world to me. He modeled true love for his own wife and family, and he understood the necessity of work and the benefit of education, though life would allow him more of the former than the latter. I recall the time he spent planning how he would achieve income and then budgeting those often meager amounts. But still he always managed a seasonal Sunday trip to the mountains, enjoyed an occasional weekend at the coast, and spent most of his time capturing every moment of his children's lives on an 8 mm camera, making sure we knew the value of memories.

Do I love my dad? Absolutely! Has he always felt loved? I can only hope so, for being the dad of a leader may have robbed him of many moments that both of us—in fact, all of us, to include my wife and daughter—would have cared to share. It occurs to me as I write that possibly these lives may have been the least served by me, and in fact their service to me may have been the only true leadership offered.

My mom, though not always understanding me, I'm sure, has in critical moments stood by me in prayer. The night when I was eleven and went crying into my parents' room, she was the one who explained to me my Eli-Samuel moment, encouraging me to return to my room and listen to the voice of God. That moment may have defined my life.

My wife has taken me to a new level of understanding and appreciation for life. She introduced me to traditions and to the meaning of "home." Christmas with her is every child's dream, a house filled with the aroma of freshly baked goods; multiple trees decorated in such a way that each deserves its own place in a magazine; and the house, as often as our lives allow, full of people. She does everything for others; her gift is hospitality, not showmanship. Well, that is also one of her gifts, but never a motive! Because she is such a creative person, our house has always been a place that people wanted to visit, both to socialize and to visualize, as every corner and every shelf strategically speaks life through her handiwork.

My daughter captured my heart from day one. Her first cry was actually a little delayed, as Dr. Green held this tiny, somewhat blue, fluid-covered being. I was privileged to cut her umbilical cord, and as the doctor handed her to me on a paperlike blanket, I stood and watched—yes, wondered—while color rushed back into her body. It had taken twenty-four hours of labor that seemed like days to expel her from her mother's womb. But with that tremendous effort, I became a daddy!

My next weeks were spent rocking this gift to sleep, singing each night, "Jesus loves this little baby. Yes, He loves this tiny baby." It was a corny little song, whose melody I alone remember, but it was my way of speaking the God love I felt. Then came the days of carrying her on my shoulders as LaDonna and I proudly walked this newcomer around the neighborhood. The older she became, the louder she sang—swinging and singing—our backyard was her amphitheater.

Those early days were short-lived, as my life seemed to be stolen away by obligations that followed opportunities to lead at church, in the public school system, and in the community. She was kind to me, at one point explaining that she missed me but that she understood! That's the love of a child.

There I was, rushing around like the Mad Hatter, arrogant enough to believe that God could use me to change lives—and, yes, even a city—but not yet humble enough to understand the real source of any lasting impact. I rushed around all day and tumbled into bed at night, striving to devise some remedy for the challenges I faced and the people I felt called to serve.

Other acknowledgments are owed to extended family and friends, like Carla Robbins, who read and edited the first manuscripts when they were yet unpublished—and this one through five iterations! Carla, I just used an exclamation mark, the very thing you warned me not to overuse!

Then there are men like Lester Burnette who was willing to listen to God and offered me a place for prayer nestled twenty-four floors above the city that I would come to love. He did this for four years, two without charge, until my business, which he advised in start-up, took a life of its own.

I would also like to acknowledge Richard Redding, now deceased, and Nancy Anders, both of whom mentored me in real estate; Merwyn Hayes who coached "this coach"; and Jim Bryan, Robby Lee, and Dr. Craig Hunt, who allowed me to share life with them. One more, though I fear I may leave out many others, is the Reverend Kevin Frack, my Moravian cohort, who unlike many pastors dared to follow Christ.

My regards as well for the coaching of Tracy Sullivan and David Looney of Xulon Press, editor Brenda Pitts and Stu Epperson, Sr. for making facilities available for the novice that I am.

# CHAPTER 1

# The Psychology and Symptoms of Foreclosure

*More than 800,000 properties received foreclosure filings in the first quarter of 2009. This is the highest number in history and is likely due to many bank moratoriums coming to an end.*

—RealtyTrac

As a fourth-generation Pentecostal believer, I am totally aware of the validity of the gift of prophecy. Nonetheless, I am also familiar with the number of false prophets who have capitalized on current events to imply some catastrophic future that aligned with their end-time theories, only to wish later that they could retrieve the books published. I certainly don't want to be numbered in that lot! I believe in America and the church of America: "God shed His grace on thee and crowned thy good with brotherhood from sea to shining sea."

Maybe I'm just a little anxious, given the economy; with my focus on foreclosures nothing more than subliminal, given that I am a licensed realtor. I'll let the reader be the judge. However, this could just as well be a demonstration of God's sovereignty in my life.

I have been working on my first book since retreating from my position as executive associate at a large church in my hometown in 1997. About that time, I became aware that even a large church might be no more successful at reaching a city than numerous small churches (even if on every corner) unless those congregants were individually engaged in serving that city. In my passion to truly be a Christ follower, I resigned what had become my second life career (my first as a public school educator) to engage in intentional prayer over our city. Opening an office on the twenty-fourth floor of our tallest downtown commercial building, I began a life-changing season of prayer. My personal needs then led me to form a small consulting company and later become a realtor. Was that vocational morphing more about preparing my mind for this book than for creating income? Again, I'll let the reader decide.

My years as a realtor have afforded numerous observations of similarities evident among most homes in foreclosure. A majority of those homes have been totally neglected, if not partially destroyed, by their previous owners. This intentional destructive behavior portends foreclosure as symptomatic of some deeper viral-like infection that eventually overcomes those who experiment with a life of unhealthy, high-risk debt as opposed to living within the principles of financial discipline and patient accumulation of resources. Somewhere in that gambler approach to life, a deterioration of self-will and a growing sense of entitlement creep in, often followed by the psychological pressures of debt, abandonment of hope, bitterness at life, and other ensuing spiritual repercussions. Fear, anger, and blame then surface in these victims of their own lusts as they are swallowed up by a life lived well beyond their means.

Lest I appear too judgmental, let me say before going further that there are certainly exceptions to this process of foreclosure. Among them are those victimized by such unfortunate situations as chronic illness, unforeseen divorce, and the unexpected loss of employment. However, it became apparent to me after a few walkthroughs as a realtor that many homeowners assumed a lifestyle of irresponsibility, leaving their homes vandalized or in filth, with appliances often ripped out or stolen in some last-minute departure prior to mailing in their keys, and finally abandoning any former covenants made with lenders. Some even reflected a more demented course of action, an "if I can't have it, you can't either" attitude that led them to knock holes in the walls and to destroy lighting fixtures.

In one case, a well-educated and previously wealthy spouse even cut all the electrical wires in her million-dollar home, as if wronged by this legal repossession process agreed upon at closing. In less destructive personalities, limited but still bizarre symptoms of failure surfaced, such as half-completed paint jobs, unfinished woodwork projects, and minor repairs ignored for months if not years before foreclosure. Something obviously was broken in the owner long before the crescendo of financial crisis.

I hope as you read through this litany of cases, you were able to draw parallels to some of the equally bizarre church episodes so common in America today. Will the church eventually react unpredictably if someone attempts to forewarn her of similar symptoms within the sanctuary, even if the warning is spoken in love? History is replete with moments when the messenger has been lost, even martyred, in moments of reform. I trust this will not be one of those times, but I must deliver, if I am to rest.

In a recent and privileged conversation with transformational author Brian McLaren, who has published such wake-up calls as *Finding Our Way Again* and *Everything Must Change: Jesus, Global Crisis, and a Revolution of Hope,* I asked what he thought might be necessary for the church to truly experience the deep change that he recommends in his own writings. His reply was swift: "Men have to die. Unless men die, religion wins!" Well said.

## Points of Reflection:

What thoughts occur regarding your own life experience within the institutional church as you read this initial chapter?

Were you moved in any particular way as you read the preface and the selected quotes from Revelation 5?

Could repossession of the institutional church by the Lord of the church be implied in Revelation 5? Why not do a brief study on the word "scroll?"

# Chapter 2

# Symptoms in the Sanctuary

*Fifty percent of all adults now contend that Christianity is just one of many options that Americans choose from and that a huge majority of adults pick and choose what they believe rather than adopt a church or denomination's slate of beliefs.*

—George Barna
August 2008 survey

Columnist Tom Ehrich offers some interesting insight into why this decline in traditional Christianity has occurred in our nation:

When this (non-attendance) slide started in 1964 as baby boomers began graduating from high school, many church leaders didn't even acknowledge it. For years, they kept counting the absent as present. Then, when the losses couldn't be ignored, they blamed them on whatever hot-button issues were roiling the religious establishment, as if new liturgies, women in leadership, and liberals (or conservatives, take your pick) had driven people away. The problem is Christianity's

31

delivery system. We are stuck in trying to lure people to physical locations at a time of our choosing, to do what we think they ought to do, and to be loyal in paying for it. It is time that we looked beyond the paradigm of Sunday church.[1]

I agree wholeheartedly with Ehrich, but my arriving at that conclusion came gradually. My first manuscript, "Kingdom Business: A Handbook of Hindsights" was begun in 1997 and is still unpublished. Originally intended as a means of capturing and communicating the things that I was beginning to sense in the midnineties, it slowly evolved into a tool for journaling and capturing my autobiography.

Though my formal training and career track was in public education, my life began changing in 1978 when I first heard the Lord promise, "Wherever I send you, seek that city; I will give you a city; if not this one (Lexington, NC) the next." Since that time, my life ambition has been to reach cities for Christ. You can see that I am somewhat of a dreamer, one who expects no small things of a life devoted to Christ!

All my life while I was growing up, my family participated in church. I was a fourth-generation Pentecostal, a relatively unknown denomination among my friends. However, my attendance in church diminished in my late teens; then, after a radical experience with God in 1973, I became involved again with ministry through an interdenominational prayer breakfast in the town where I was employed as a classroom teacher. This soon led to my wife's and my participation in a small church that nurtured our new Christian lifestyle and provided leadership opportunities.

Eventually I was encouraged to make a professional career change as a means of fulfilling my ministry ambitions. The majority of my full-time pastoral experience that followed was in service to a large church, a megachurch in the eyes of those who watched it grow from thirteen members in a basement to thirty-five hundred on a campus adjoining one of the nation's premier universities.

However, it required only six years in a full-time pastoral role for me to realize that what had been recommended to me by denominational leaders as a means of reaching cities—that is, a large church— no longer seemed to be the tool that God wanted to use to fulfill my life ambition. My life soon became totally concerned with kingdom business—not my book, but rather a lifestyle that is more about the kingdom than about income production or church-based ministry.

What does this have to do with my writing? It was that experience of life transition from a professional educator and administrator to an assistant pastor, then church consultant, pastoral coach, and entrepreneur that kept morphing my book for over a decade. That journey brought me to a place of conviction that doing church better should no longer be a kingdom aspiration—at least for me. After all, it's not about doing church, but about being Christ!

This book is about sharing the observations of that journey as a means of freeing those souls still trapped within dysfunctional churches. It is affirming what many are now sensing: that there is a life in Christ outside the church, and at best, church is a place to celebrate with those of similar beliefs what God has done through one's life in the marketplace. At worst, church has become a containment strategy to keep believers out of the marketplace and segregated from the greater body of Christ, a less-than-effective means of sharing the good news of Jesus Christ and a sinkhole for otherwise better-used kingdom capital.

With church attendance in decline, first in the Northwest and now slowly creeping toward the Bible Belt, churches have little excuse for being caught off guard. Years of diminishing freedom of Christian expression within our nation and the rapid moral decline now impacting even our economy should have warned discerning leadership of the church's ineffectiveness, just as notices from creditors forewarn homeowners of impending peril and foreclosure. In addition, the emotional struggles within congregations, the divisions between denominations, and even the daily stressful challenges of pastoral leadership should cause us pause and create a need to reexamine our spiritual household before the final summons is delivered to our door.

My objective is not to scorn the church; however, neither can I avoid the truth regarding its current ineffectiveness. When I reflect on being churched all these years, I find myself wanting to retreat from everything and focus on knowing Christ alone, for I sense that in my serving the church, I have fallen short on knowing the Christ. Yet when I seek to withdraw, I hear the voice of God cautioning me not to neglect the body of Christ, and the urgent need for transformation confronts me even more.

True, God's promises are unchanging, but given the epochal time of transformation in which we live, the institutional church must change. As is becoming apparent to many who seek radical transformation, the challenge in all of our systems is the requirement of major life adjustments among leaders, even a redistribution of wealth, which we tend to avoid at all means.

Ignoring the radical changes necessary in our churches is like knowing there is a slow leak in the concrete backyard pool that will eventually require repairs but continuing to refill it each summer because the water is just too comfortable as it is. That's exactly what we do in church. We keep filling it up, freshening it up, and quick-fixing for each new generation, hoping the main leak will fix itself. Meanwhile, the infrastructure and foundational grounding continue to erode.

Without a doubt, it will require great courage to not only address the problem but to also take the steps necessary to correct it. I think Thomas Merton expressed it well:

1. There can be no doubt, no compromise, in my decision to be completely faithful to God's will and truth, and hence I must seek always and in everything to act for His will and in His truth, and thus to seek with His grace to be "a saint."

2. There must be no doubt, no compromise in my efforts to avoid falsifying this work of truth by considering too much what others approve of and regard as "holy." In a word, it may happen (or may not) that what God demands of me may

make me look less perfect to others, and that it may rob me of their support, their affection, their respect. To become a saint therefore may mean the anguish of looking like, and in a real sense "being," a sinner, an outcast. It may mean apparent conflict with certain standards that may be wrongly understood by me or by others or by all of us.

3. The thing is to cling to God's will and truth in their purity and try to be sincere and to act in all things out of genuine love, in so far as I can.[2]

How long has the church in America been headed for foreclosure? Are there subtle signs in our sanctuaries that should be visited, signs of foundational neglect within our institutions? Do the challenges now facing the nations of our world find their root causes at the feet of those failed institutions? There are indeed multiple leaks in this pool, some of which I will now attempt in grace to articulate constructively.

"The psalmist declares in Psalm 119, 'Your promises have been thoroughly tested, and your servant loves them.' Reaching through generation after generation, the laws of God stand untouched and unfazed by changing environments. Again and again, God's servants discover a reason to love the ways and promises of God, to draw near the truth and beauty in the ageless presence of a God who is both love and wisdom. 'I learned from your statutes that you established them to last forever' (Psalm 119:152). In times when levels of uncertainty seem toxic and the decay of hope unremitting, God's presence is the ultimate preservative. God's words were not spoken without meaning; God's purposes are filled with the intention of life. God's promises have been thoroughly tested and have yet to expire."[3]

## Points of Reflection:

Are sentiments and emotions stirred within you as you continue to read?
Take a moment to record your thoughts.

What do your answers imply about your love for the church or its need for change?

Did you find the word 'foreclosure' appropriate to the change process now evident in churches?

Reflecting on current socio-economic changes occurring across our globe, what necessary response do you sense might be in store for the church?

# CHAPTER 3

# Prophets of Prosperity

*The consequences of iniquities will find us out, this is an eternal principle which governs the righteousness of God and His judgment is fair. As God used the wicked Babylonians to judge Judah and Israel, so God will use the system outside of the Church to judge them, if the Church is incapable to do so.*

-Daniel, Danski.wordpress.com

I recall a recent Sunday morning as I held the remote, channel surfing as a means of combating boredom in one of my sporadic early-morning treadmill ventures. Before my eyes was a local pastor whom I knew, emotionally charged with towel in hand, mimicking a more popular televangelist as he wiped sweat from his brow in between outbursts of "revelation" that assured his congregation of their soon-coming financial blessing. Familiar with this "brother" and bored with running in place, I decided to listen in.

While observing these shenanigans, I believe the Lord whispered these words to me: *spiritual lottery.*

There before this minister was a room packed full of deceived believers hoping that by bringing their offerings to that church alone, they would reap a windfall. At the same time, I would venture, the pastor who controlled the deposits was likely the only one in that congregation driving a Mercedes. The storehouse to which the people's tithes were delivered was simply a franchise through which this "brother" made his living!

This is what the Lord says: "You false prophets are leading my people astray! You promise peace for those who give you food, but you declare war on those who refuse to feed you. Now the night will close around you, cutting off all your visions. Darkness will cover you, putting an end to your predictions. The sun will set for you prophets, and your day will come to an end. Then you seers will be put to shame, and you fortune-tellers will be disgraced. And you will cover your faces because there is no answer from God."

But as for me, I am filled with power—with the Spirit of the Lord. I am filled with justice and strength to boldly declare Israel's sin and rebellion.

Listen to me, you leaders of Israel! You hate justice and twist all that is right. You are building Jerusalem on a foundation of murder and corruption. You rulers make decisions based on bribes; you priests teach God's laws only for a price; you prophets won't prophesy unless you are paid. Yet all of you claim to depend on the Lord. "No harm can come to us," you say, "for the Lord is here among us." Because of you, Mount Zion

will be plowed like an open field; Jerusalem will
be reduced to ruins! A thicket will grow on the
heights where the Temple now stands.
                                    —Micah 3:5–12 NLT


Both the Old and New Testament provide warn-
ings and direct contrasts to misguided churches such
as described above: "Whatever you give is acceptable if you give it eagerly. And give according to
what you have, not what you don't have. Of course,
I don't mean your giving should make life easy for
others and hard for yourselves. I only mean that
there should be some equality. Right now you have
plenty and can help those who are in need. Later,
they will have plenty and can share with you when
you need it. In this way, things will be equal" (2 Cor.
8:12–14 NLT).

How can anyone read Scriptures such as the one
from 2 Corinthians yet believe in the existence of
churches that condone disparity within their own
congregations in the name of capitalism and exhibit
blindness for social justice within the community
while holding real estate on almost every corner? Yet
the ministers of those same churches applaud the early
church for its decision to hold all things common,
implying that everything should be submitted to
church leadership, as in the book of Acts. Something
is terribly twisted in our practice of the gospel!

Outside the church, while we have been busy
attending to this gospel of personal prosperity, we
have totally neglected our responsibility for the community. Consequently, the government has been positioned by default to do what should be the mission of

the church. Ignoring the balance of equality and social justice, the church has perpetuated a national sense of entitlement to abundance through the preaching of the prosperity message.

In today's Americanized culture, man's love for wealth may have finally exceeded his sense of stewardship. Even our physical environment and its phenomenal ecological systems have become as neglected as in any time in our world's history. Fortunately, not only was the earth designed to cleanse itself from natural wastes, but it was also provided with some margin for catastrophic elements. Though natural ecological cycles constantly cleanse our atmosphere and our aquatic systems, mankind's impact over the centuries has become increasingly evident and progressively burdensome. We have raped our natural resources and nearly exhausted our fuel supplies. We now sit on the brink of disaster from global warming as our ice caps melt and dilute the balance of saltwater necessary for marine life, while at the same time human sewage and agricultural runoff create dead zones in our estuaries, ultimately destroying the very oceans once designed for replenishing the oxygen critical to our survival.

Christians are the stewards of the earth. When we violate this sacred covenant for the sake of wealth and our lustful desire for comfort and pleasure, the kingdom of God is in peril, not because God is not in control if need be, but because He has entrusted the vineyard to us (Mark 12:1–3). We are His tenant farmers!

"There is also the nonecology: the destructive unbalance of nature, poisoned and unsettled by bombs, by fallout, by exploitation: the land ruined, the waters contaminated, the soil charged with chemicals, ravaged with machinery, the houses of farmers falling apart because everybody goes to the city and stays there. There is no poverty as great as that of the prosperous, no wretchedness as dismal as affluence. Wealth is poison. There is no misery to compare with that, which exists where technology has been a total success. Full bellies have not brought peace and satisfaction but dementia, and, in any case, not all the bellies are full. But the dementia is the same for all."[1]

In our nation, materialistic lust has created an uncontrolled sprawl, pushing remaining land to the limits in food production. Imports of oil to fuel our transportation, along with the consumption of our world's forest for the construction of "McMansions" has created a nation that consumes grossly disproportionate amounts of the earth's resources. We have one of the world's most thriving economies and enviable lifestyles (the attempted bailouts in 2008–09 may change all that), but we are rapidly becoming a detriment to other developing countries, many of which are becoming less and less enchanted by this American life that once could boast of true Christianity.

This imbalance of economic prosperity and disregard for environmental sustainability continues to be propagated by sociopolitical systems that are more about power and greed than wisdom and benevolence. Our families are fragmented, even within the church community. Marriage is in decline, and children are producing children out of wedlock at staggering rates.

Our streets are littered with the fallout of bereft social systems, and our cities struggle with chronic homelessness and growing gang activity. Meanwhile, the huge gap widens between the haves and the have-nots, with a gnawing awareness of the future impact of a burgeoning population on our globe.

America's prison population is bursting at the seams as society fails at social justice, and with that failure comes the depletion of resources that once provided a second-to-none educational experience by way of our public schools and universities. Both China and India, our greatest emerging competitors, now produce more engineers than the United States and, I am told, house more students in their gifted programs than we have in our entire system! Our universities and schools are less and less the place to nurture future leadership and creativity. As our educational institutions fall behind, many churches, some the original founders of these same educational institutions, have become irrelevant religious facilities that are more about sustaining obsolete real estate than bringing truth and light at this most desperate time.

My hometown of Winston-Salem is known for underwear (Hanes), tobacco (R. J. Reynolds) and doughnuts (Krispy Kreme). Krispy Kreme became one of the Wall Street darlings in early 2000, only to be racked with failure later on because of over-franchising and poor management. "Now hot" neon signs once attracted customers into minimal-space stores with conveyor belts full of round carbohydrate-laden treats coated with a rich, sugary glaze. This culinary rage set off the capitalistic nature of the company's leaders at that time and soon morphed into a franchise of greed, racing toward market in a way that soon led to calamity for a Cinderella story once famed for its goodness and philanthropic leadership in its founding city (see *Making Dough* by Kirk Kazanjian and Amy Joyner).

This marketplace reflection is offered as a metaphor, used recently by the Lord as I was driving through a neighborhood known for its challenges, causing me to compare the many small churches visible in that neighborhood to the challenges once faced by Krispy Kreme. These churches represent an overly franchised industry of goodness, each with diminished stock value. Yet they are found on almost every street corner, virtually empty and void of impact at least six days a week.

Many of these religious franchises have become part of an industry supported by frequent emotional revivals that fail to deliver more than mere promises of true spiritual benefit to others. These small-time CEO/pastors personally participate in disproportionate financial prosperity and spend otherwise beneficial contributions on the upkeep of obsolete buildings from which they extract a living. In the name of God, these churches annually remove relatively large amounts of resources from already underresourced communities, and their pastors often live in other parts of the city or even in other towns. Valuable resources are squandered that might otherwise be used to aid indigent families, as in the case of this one community where approximately twelve hundred previously incarcerated individuals return each year without hope or remedy as they reenter society. Recently I asked that these locations be plotted on a map alongside their community-crime data, and to my surprise crime was more concentrated around the churches. Some might interpret this as symptomatic of spiritual warfare — I would call it ineffectiveness.

As a stockholder, and devout addict of these locally-based deep-fried, delicious treats, I would need to point out that Krispy Kreme's new leadership has done much to redeem this locally based enterprise. A dozen Krispy Kremes still go a long way in positioning one well at any gathering!

The good news for the church is that our looming economic crisis, as will be the case in other industries, may soon eliminate the weakest of these franchises and thus free kingdom resources for true community ministry. If not, providing energy for all these facilities may soon become unconscionable, if not unlawful. Churches initially were minimal and served more of a collective function, celebrating the goodness of God as men and women used their gifts and their businesses to enable true community. As society grew and individuals from various belief systems demanded their own spaces, the institutional church experienced the same bubble as other industries and is now out of balance, and, in fact, out of touch with the realities of this world.

I am cautious about criticism that offers no solutions, so just how would an individual apart from a church approach ministry? First, every human being has been given some measure of faith, some ray of hope, some dream for life, a voice heard within the mother's womb. That is readily visible in the eyes of every newborn child, assuming that life has not been preempted by parental substance abuse or other prenatal challenges. I like to refer to this innate gift, this calling, as *spiritual capital,* a voice that if cultivated will manifest in a vocation that adds value to one's community.

I also believe God's will is to position each and every person with purpose and that each life is truly unique. Each time we meet a new person, we meet a new piece of God. We should reverence that uniqueness, understanding that each life represents a piece of God never to be assigned to another, for He is truly inexhaustible. That uniqueness is a person's *human capital,* the talents, skills, and abilities held intact by precious DNA. Yes, to some degree I understand the random challenges of genetics, but I also understand an omnipotent God whose sovereignty broods over the embryo and "creates no junk" when the womb, a sacred tabernacle, is left undefiled and protected.

As God favors our lives and we nurture relationship with Him, our spiritual capital is increased, and our human capital is thus enhanced in value. Our lives eventually will attract *financial capital* as our lives find voice and our vocations unfold. This may be where the prosperity doctrine and capitalism have caused us to leave the principles of Christ. Yes, we acquire wealth, but we are only stewards of that wealth, wise investors who seek a return as reflected in the proverbs of Christ. Wealth is certainly not for accumulation alone or to create successive generations where each has more wealth than those who preceded them.

To simplify, this is how I visualize the interconnectedness and purpose of each facet of God's plan for each of His children:

God provides
*Spiritual capital* (a measure of faith)
To enhance your
*Human capital* (talents, skills, abilities)
To generate and attract
*Financial capital*
To be stewarded toward
*Philanthropic capital*
For the sake of
*Ministry*
Through which we bless others for
His glorification and have
*Abundant life!*

Jesus came that we might have life and have it more abundantly—true life, the love of life, philanthropy. Philanthropy is about ministry to others, caring for one another, engaging our lives in community. His kingdom economy is neither capitalism nor socialism; it is about each life adding value to the lives of others and each life receiving value as it serves others. For the one who knows abundant life, true ministry does not happen only in or near churches, but rather in real-time relationships, seven days a week. That is far from the current lifestyle of the typical American churchgoer or at least the average churchgoer that I know.

Unless we once again return to the principles of the kingdom, the entire church industry as we now know it may be at risk.

## Points of Reflection:

Why not pause for a moment of self-evaluation regarding your own personal prosperity? Better yet, why not record your blessings as a means of thanksgiving?

What is your opinion of the American church and the prosperity gospel when you reflect on the existing needs of believers in other countries?

Where do you spend the majority of your focus, building spiritual capital or financial?

Reflect on your own generosity and philanthropy as compared to the blessings you have experienced in Christ?

# CHAPTER 4

# A God That Is Tame

*If Jesus has come to dwell within you, you are no longer suited for a normal life. To have the Spirit of God dwelling within the heart of someone who chooses a domesticated faith is like having a tiger trapped in a cage.*

—Erwin Raphael McManus
*The Barbarian Way*

In Ezekiel 24:16, God instructed the prophet with these words: "Son of man, behold, I take away from thee the desire of thine eyes [Ezekiel's wife] with a stroke; yet neither shalt thou mourn nor weep, neither shall thy tears run down." When I read verses like this, I often think of C. S. Lewis's words in The Lion, the Witch, and the Wardrobe in a conversation concerning the great Aslan:

> "Aslan is a lion—*the* Lion, the great Lion."
> "Ooh!" said Susan, "I'd thought he was a man. Is he—quite safe? I shall feel rather nervous about meeting a lion."

"That you will, dearie, and no mistake," said Mrs. Beaver; "if there's anyone who can appear before Aslan without their knees knocking, they're either braver than most or else just silly."

"Then he isn't safe?" said Lucy.

"Safe?" said Mr. Beaver; "don't you hear what Mrs. Beaver tells you? Who said anything about safe? 'Course he isn't safe. But he's good. He's the King I tell you."[1]

Is He safe? Ask Ezekiel. God is not safe; but as C. S. Lewis reminds us, He is good.

We love the soft side of God, cheap grace some call it: "The Lord is my shepherd, I shall not want." Unfortunately, however, in the American church the words often become more directive toward God: "I better not want!"

In his writing of the Twenty-third Psalm, David was certainly accurate; even Jesus who was God said, "I am the good Shepherd," but life has its seasons and sheep have a life cycle. The good shepherd of David's day raised sheep not only with the goal of physical provision for his family but also with the aspiration of annually raising a firstborn male lamb with no blemish. That perfect lamb had no want because the shepherd cared for, guarded, and even caressed that special lamb, knowing that one day it would enter the sacrificial sheep gate.

I am told that in the ancient walls of Jerusalem, there was a gate on the north side through which the animals were brought in from the countryside for sacrifice. This gate was called the Sheep Gate. Once inside the city and within the temple courts, no lamb ever went back out. The lambs traveled in only one direction, and from their point of entrance, they were destined toward sacrifice for the sins of men and women. The entrance gate was narrow, and only a good, skilled shepherd could guide worthy sheep to and through the gate. Those small gentle animals, which had earlier been so cared for, must have sensed death on the other side of the gate; yet because of their deep trust in the good shepherd, they walked through the valley of the shadow of death and feared no evil. The same shepherd guiding them through the gate would certainly lay down his life for them, and many did.

Jesus said, "I am the door, the gate." Yes, He is the sheep gate, the narrow gate, the gate through which only the select could enter, but through which none returned. We too are lambs destined for the slaughter! For first-century hearers of Jesus' words about sheep, such knowledge added to the shock of Christ's words: "I tell you the truth, I am the door . . . the gate for the sheep . . . whoever enters through me will be saved." He goes on to say, "He shall go in and out and find pasture" (John 10:7, 9 paraphrased). Some irony may be found here, as the Sheep Gate theretofore afforded only death, yet the sheep that Christ spoke of could go in and out. In and out of what? I suspect, the kingdom of God on and within this Earth!

In John 5:24, Jesus gives us an answer: "I tell you the truth, whoever hears my word and believes him who sent me has eternal life and will not be condemned; he has crossed over from death to life" (MSG). Jesus is the gate, but this gate, rather than providing death to the living sheep, provides life to the dead. We are all dead in our trespasses and sins, yet in our blindness we think we live. Jesus at Calvary provided sight for the blind, but the journey there relative to what we call life appears as death, for we in fact must die to this world. However, the gospel implies that in dying we find life.

These paradoxical statements are similar to other comments Jesus made to His disciples, such as when they brought food to Him as recorded in John 4:32. "I have meat to eat that you know not of," He said. He had come from the kingdom and already knew how to live there! Is He safe? Never! Is life with Him good? Absolutely!

What is this terrible but good God saying to His church? I believe He says, "Greater love has no man than to lay down his life for his friends." The God we serve is not the savage god of 9/11, but the God who presses our lives toward a narrow gate for the sake of those who have not yet had that love affirmed. It is not His will that any should perish, but that all should come to know true life in Christ. We, the people of God, His church, must die that they who are perishing might come to know life through the salt and light of our lives. It is therefore imperative that we first die.

The key mission of the church can certainly not be abundance or prosperity alone; it may actually be death. Jesus Himself told us, "I tell you the truth, unless a kernel of wheat is planted in the soil and dies, it remains alone. But its death will produce many new kernels, a plentiful harvest of new lives. Those who love their life in this world will lose it. Those who care nothing for their life in this world will keep it for eternity. Anyone who wants to be my disciple must follow me, because my servants must be where I am. And the Father will honor anyone who serves me" (John 12:24–26 NLT).

"For thy sake we are killed all the day long; we are accounted as sheep for the *slaughter*" (Rom. 8:36, emphasis added). This is no tame God, the one who became flesh that early morning as a babe in Bethlehem! Neither is our life with Him solely about Christmas or escaping the tribulation and challenges of this world: "In this world you will have tribulation, but be of good cheer; I have overcome the world" (John 16:33). Our life and our obligation to Him are all about others, presenting our lives as "a living sacrifice wholly and acceptable to God, our reasonable service" (Rom. 12:1–2).

Like a house that has fallen into disrepair, when a church has lost the message of sacrifice, it has lost its salt and is good only for the dung heap.

## Points of Reflection:

Do these words of sacrifice and suffering seem foreign to the message of American Christianity?

Does the mandate of Romans 8:36 still apply to believers today?

What requirements are implied by that mandate?

Take a moment to read the remainder of Romans 8, then reflect on what God might be speaking to you personally.

# CHAPTER 5

# A God Who No Longer Speaks

*For this people's heart has become calloused; they hardly hear with their ears, and they have closed their eyes. Otherwise they might see with their eyes, hear with their ears, understand with their hearts and turn, and I would heal them.*

—Acts 28:27 NIV

Another of the more obvious symptoms of impending spiritual foreclosure is the loss of desire to truly hear or know God, no longer awed by whom He is or the stories He writes with our lives. This is a far cry from the passion described by the lover in the Song of Solomon or the psalmist who longs after Him as the deer pants for the water brooks. Unfortunately, many of us read Scripture almost as if it were fantasy, with little desire to have the kind of God journey that it offers.

This loss of awe within our churches is fed by the constant disclaimers of professional clergy and "learned" laymen alike who offer caution in interpreting the irrational prophets of the Bible and their words from long ago. Substituting a God more akin to Santa Claus, they replace the God of Scripture with a mute, powerless God whose sole purpose is man's comfort. Prayer is reduced to a religious exercise, and even among those who do believe, prayer is little more than the recitation of a wish list. We have allowed the ranks of clergy to be infiltrated by prophets of prosperity who promise abundance in response to faithful service to their churches while enhancing donations to their own individual franchises of religion. Meanwhile, the demonstration of a living God is seldom witnessed in the churches of America, even in the midst of this propped-up prosperity.

I believe in tithing, and I do believe that I am blessed because of it. But abundance and blessing are relative to where God desires to position us in life, which, by the way, is His call. True abundance is the ability to live and love wherever He places us socioeconomically and seasonally, as well as the ability to serve and to lead with the grace and the power of God those who are unloving, look different, smell different, or even love differently.

It has always puzzled me how many clergy, posturing themselves as apostles, prophets, pastors, teachers, and evangelists, hedge on having heard the voice of God or, in some cases, are unable to cite any supernatural intervention in their own lives beyond their call to ministry. Even their call, in many cases, was actually nothing more than professional preparation and the natural progression through a denominational system that moves its managers over time and rewards faithful service with upward mobility, as would any industry. Meanwhile, these same clergy attempt to impassion congregants with the words from ancient men of faith like Jeremiah, Isaiah, and Ezekiel, who, they say, did hear from God and did in fact do exploits (Dan. 11:32). That same Word states that God never changes, yet they recoil when someone from within their ranks claims to have heard from God and are quick to explain away the miraculous when a parishioner does have a spiritual moment! What's with that?

Does God speak? Absolutely! Can He be heard by the average Joe? You bet! In fact, I believe that I have heard Him multiple times. My first memory of a vocal encounter with God occurred when I was nine. I vividly remember the moment and even where I sat on that small embankment beside a large well-trimmed hedge alongside Tech Boulevard on the south side of Winston-Salem, North Carolina. I clearly heard an audible voice say to me, "One day you will preach the gospel."

Why God spoke to me in that moment I do not know. I was not seated in some Sunday school class contemplating a Bible story, nor was I returning from some fiery youth camp; rather, I was resting from the hard play of cowboys and Indians with my friend Greg Carlyle. I must say that my attempts at reentering play were difficult after that, as I recall being stunned by the realization of what had just happened. My life would never be the same.

Though I believe I always knew it was God's voice, it was not until later that it was reaffirmed in a dream I had at the age of eleven. Awakened one night by the sound of phenomenal high-church music, unlike any music I had been exposed to thus far, I sat up in bed in awe. I lay awake for some time, literally looking up at some windowlike opening into heaven well beyond the ceiling of my bedroom. Yes, this future mayor was having a vision. Frightened by this surreal experience, I ran crying into my parents' bedroom, only to have my mom, who discerned a Samuel-Eli moment, encourage me to return to bed and listen to what the Lord might be saying.

How do I know it was God? Now, almost fifty years later, He has guarded that word providentially, added to that word experientially, and made real much of that vision to date, even though at times I have sinfully disregarded His plans and purposes, even attempting to flee from that word in Jonah-like moments of rebellion.

Who can understand this terrible God first time around? Every person's life is limited by the leadership around him or her, parental or otherwise. Like so many others, I was raised in the context of a small church, and the people with whom my family and I worshiped tended to attract only those who chose to act and believe like us. This may have been the greatest error of my devoted parents and the greatest tool of the evil one. In their sincere attempt to please the church, my parents, who often heard God's voice, may have listened more at times to those positioned by the church than to the voice within.

My parents did recognize the authority of pastors and other leaders to offer the word of the Lord for their family but held those men and women accountable for allowing the full work of the Holy Spirit within our particular body of believers. For that I am thankful, as many of my friends were not as fortunate. Many of them experienced neither parents in true relationship with Christ nor the manifestation of miracles that I came to accept as commonplace. Many of their churches were already well down the road toward foreclosure when it came to any vibrant expression of the Holy Spirit.

Nevertheless, as unintentional as it was, our lives were often segregated from the greater body of Christ, the only true context for interpreting His Word. I believe every city has its *church,* as well as its "churches," a sort of grace menu for believers. If we spent more time together as the church, the body of Christ, might our churches also be healthier? Yet it seems that as we struggle with the work God does among us, too often we find the need to plant new churches when our current work of God becomes too much of a challenge for us to get along. I thought it somewhat humorous when I first realized that the word *congregation* as used in Acts 13:43 is derived from a Greek term that means "a place of struggle." Think about that!

How can we know when we have heard from God? That voice should add value and worth to our life dreams, bending dreams outward toward others rather than inward toward self. It will not conflict with the principles reflected by the life of Christ—unless, of course, our interpretation of those principles is more just that than true revelation.

True revelation through His Word has a way of narrowing our list of rules. In actuality, He has already narrowed it to only two: "Jesus said unto him, Thou shalt love the Lord thy God with all thy heart, and with all thy soul, and with all thy mind. This is the first and great commandment. And the second is like unto it, Thou shalt love thy neighbor as thyself. On these two commandments hang all the law and the prophets" (Matt. 22:37–40). His rules are few and His voice can be heard, as He connects the dots of our life experiences, our play as a child, our present joys and present pains, and even our failures, working everything for our good as we know Him and journey with Him (Rom. 8:28, my version).

Hearing from God and integrating His words into our lives are values that must be retained if our individual households are to be whole and our churches spiritually solvent. When this is not the case, attending church more often, doing church better, or even employing new staff will not pay the spiritual mortgage God requires.

## Points of Reflection:

Do you ever recall God speaking to you? If so, what was He saying?

If in fact God has spoken to you, what evidence have you seen that affirms that voice?

Are you offended at the thought that one might claim to have heard from God?
Wherein might that offence be rooted?

You possibly are 'wired' quite differently from this author, if so, think of other ways God has communicated with you?

Think about this, if He has communicated to you in some other way, then have you not also heard from God? Why not try opening your other senses more to His Spirit.

## Chapter 6

# Prayer, a Mere
# Religious Exercise

*Prayer becomes a weapon that can painfully turn in on us.*

—James Houston
*The Transformed Friendship*

Prayer can be dangerous, when embraced as something more than ritual or some institutionally prescribed spiritual exercise. James Houston expresses this thought even more powerfully:

> We will find prayer a dangerous experience if we are unwilling to change. To pray is rather like joining an underground resistance movement in an enemy-occupied country. We fight back in prayer to overthrow the kingdom of darkness with the light of the gospel.
>
> The problem is that the darkness is not simply all around us, but inside us too. So prayer becomes a weapon *that can painfully turn in on us.* Prayer opposes

everything in us that is false, evil and sinful. Prayer attacks all the indifference and moral complacency, all the conceit and selfishness within us (emphasis added). [1]

It was prayer that turned on me and prayer that reorganized my life when I first determined to pursue a word spoken to my heart while standing in the front yard of my home in 1978. I found myself in dialogue with God regarding what I was reading in His Word and what I was hearing in my church. As I pondered the reality that the early church was no longer about building temples but rather about reaching cities, I heard Him speak: "Wherever I send you, seek the good of that city, if not this city the next, but I will give you a city." Though His calling had been first spoken to me as a child, the word developed more strongly over time and then in 1978 became clear as a life mission. The window of time between 1978 and 1995 better positioned my life for prayer and engagement in cities, although my full commitment to the vision was not made until February of 1997. Fortunately, a journal given to me by my wife in 1986 allowed me to capture milestones on this journey.

On a Tuesday morning in 1995, I heard the voice of the Lord during a staff devotion in which one of our children's pastors read from Jeremiah 1:7–19. I heard His voice above the pastor's, saying, "You are no longer a child." As I returned to my office, I reread some of those same verses and again heard Him calling me to a higher dimension of ministry: "Then the LORD put forth his hand, and touched my mouth. And the LORD said unto me, Behold, I have put my words in thy mouth. See, I have this day set thee over the nations and over the kingdoms, to root out, and to pull down, and to destroy, and to throw down, to build, and to plant" (vv. 9–10). I continued reading and came to verse 17: "Thou therefore gird up thy loins, and arise, and speak unto them all that I command thee: be not dismayed at their faces, lest I confound thee before them."

Later, while taking a short walk just to be alone with God, I asked Him to clarify what He might be asking me to do. He spoke these words: "When the church [body of Christ] is ready, I will take the props from under this city and open to the church the windows of heaven, and men and women will run into it; that is what you are here for." Though He ended the sentence with a preposition, that is what I heard! Once more, I recalled the vision from my childhood, that open window toward heaven, and I understood that it was time to seek the Lord and to pray toward that end.

After much prayer, I resigned from my leadership role on the church staff in 1996 with an enhanced sense of the need to physically pray over our city. My senior pastor asked the hard questions, such as how I intended to feed my family and pay for a new home then under construction. I had no quick answers, but I had made a decision based on a growing trust in that voice first heard as a child. Later God would answer those questions as I developed a ministry of pastoral coaching among the various denominations within our region. Pivotal in my growing passion for transformation of the church at large, this window of experience and the following ten years of transition allowed me to serve four senior pastors within my home church alone. Hopefully, that will assure my readership that I have not been the maverick that so many pastors fear!

In the summer of 1996, I was sitting in a parking lot as I waited for my daughter to apply for a passport for her first mission trip. "God," I asked, "where do You want me to be located?" In that same voice that I had now come to recognize, He immediately replied, "Ask Lester for an office." At that time, Lester Burnette managed the former Wachovia Building, now the Winston Towers, which stood directly across from the courthouse where I was parked. Frankly, I was shocked by God's immediate and clear response, and even more, I was hesitant to confront this local businessman whom I had come to admire. I would approach this conversation with great consternation.

The next weekend as I was teaching a Sunday school lesson, I shared the story of the famine in Samaria that took place during Elisha's lifetime. At that time the people of God were surviving off a diet of dove dung and donkey heads. Elisha then prophesied that "tomorrow about this time" the Lord would open the "windows of heaven." Four lepers, starving outside the gates of the city, determined to take the challenge. "Why sit we here until we die? If we say, We will enter into the city, then the famine is in the city, and we shall die there: and if we sit still here, we die also" (2 Kings 7:3–4). They decided to risk it all and to press into the enemy's camp, even if it meant surrender or, worse yet, death!

Just as I shared that part of the story, I heard the Lord speak to me and even found myself prophesying to the class, "Tomorrow about this time"—looking up at the classroom clock, I noticed it was 10:50 a.m.—"the Lord will open the windows of heaven for someone in this class." That night I wrestled with the Lord concerning that message and what I may have spoken into someone's life. Though it was in the early hours of the morning, I found myself in earnest prayer regarding my calling to the city.

Sometime after daylight, I realized that the Sunday school prophecy may have actually been for me. Was this the beginning of the vision I had seen as a child, that window of heaven? Recalling the Lord's earlier instruction, I called Lester's office sometime after eight on Monday morning, excited about what I thought the Lord was speaking. However, the response from Lester's secretary soon wilted my enthusiasm. After my second attempt to contact Lester, she informed me sharply that Lester seldom came into the office on Mondays. I sheepishly requested that she have him call me if he did come by that day.

About eleven o'clock (I would love to say 10:50), my secretary called to inform me that Lester Burnette had just called. I was so excited that I hung up the phone with little instruction and rushed from where I was consulting at the Living Water Family Resource Center to meet with him. When I arrived at his office on the twenty-second floor in the Wachovia Building, his secretary once again informed me that Lester did not come into the office on Mondays and that, in fact, he had notified her of another meeting with someone at a church called First Assembly of God. That was my church, and he was at my office, though his secretary was not aware of it. I then knew God was up to something and hurried to the church, where I found Lester awaiting my arrival. He had simply felt the need to meet with me that day in order to pick up a previous conversation regarding a Christian high school. God is awesome.

Not wasting any of the precious time I might have with this man, I blurted out, "Mr. Burnette, you might think that the cheese has slipped off my cracker, but I believe that God wants me to have an office in your building, preferably on a vacant floor, where I might pray over this city."

As I continued talking about my burden to reach our city, struggling to articulate my Joseph-sized dream in a believable way, Lester stopped me long enough to ask, "Will you need a phone?" He was already there. He arranged to meet me in his office the following Thursday.

When I arrived, after being offered some very meaningful advice as to how I might approach my dream, Lester took me to a fully-glassed corner office on the twenty-fourth floor, which I now believe to be those windows of heaven seen earlier in my vision. There, in an exquisitely furnished executive office, I would spend the next four years praying for a city, two of which were lease free because of Lester's heart for God. The next ten years of my life were spent gaining perspective and watching God answer those prayers.

My company, Master Counsel, Inc., a name I had also heard in prayer in 1995, was chartered in January of 1996 as a small consulting/coaching business and eventually birthed three other businesses to meet the needs of my own family as well as others. Lester's advice and mentoring over the years was critical to my success in kingdom business.

The mission to pray for my city, however, was short-lived, for within months I realized that it was for me that the Holy Spirit had called me to prayer. It was out of His intercession from deep within my belly that my own sin was uncovered and my life transformed. Out of that transformation came the stark realization of just how desperate mankind is for God and how unrighteous we religious folk truly are. The benefit of four years spent in prayer for the city proved to be more mine than that of our municipality.

I picked up many priceless lessons in those years. I learned that prayer wrestles with us daily, pinning down our religious thoughts and holding them up against the God revealed only by the Spirit. As we pursue this path of prayer, God can no longer be the simple God of our childhood, a tame God best suited for flannel-graph Sunday school stories. Through prayer, He becomes much wilder than the God of the American church, that God now more academic and sophisticated than real.

I often wrestle with what we have done with the Scriptures and the principles of Christ when I compare the lives and prayers of today's Christians against those of early Christ followers as recorded in the sacred texts. Those early believers literally turned their cities upside down, working miracles and mighty works theretofore seen only at the hands of the Christ. This paragraph and much of this book may sound judgmental and might bear Jesus' warning "Judge not and ye shall not be judged," yet serious review of Scriptures like these do not imply that we should be fearful of speaking out when the principles of Scripture are violated. Jesus' and Paul's admonitions regarding judgment were meant to caution believers tempted to judge or point fingers at "real sinners" as a means of denying their own sins. Examination of Scriptures like 1 Corinthians 5:1–13 will conclude that the church is not above being judged by those within it, God alone judging those outside the church.

For some time now, my generation has been asleep at the wheel, engaging in fervent prayer only when hidden within the walls of our sanctuaries and offering only sterile public prayer that is more suitable for ball games and political gatherings. Our impotence has alienated the next generation, one which might gladly reenter the Father's house with new energy, new passion, and new desire if they could once more witness the Ancient of Days among our rituals. Yes, they would come clothed in a way that disavows our prosperity doctrine, as some tried earlier with their grunge wear, then cheap bling, and now with skin wrapped in "tats" of indelible ink and flesh pierced in places that pain their elders. Yet the reality is that what we have called sacred has in the absence of true prayer become nothing more than rank ritual, followed by silence from a God no longer welcome in our conversations. Thank God for a generation crying out with their lives in true hope of finding the God we have only professed!

I trust this book does become an axe for any frozen seas within your life and that true prayer once more begins to burn white-hot in your own heart. I pray, in fact, that prayer turns on you and that you will then turn on the churches of your city until righteousness reigns once more in our nation and Christ truly repossesses His church.

## Points of Reflection:

Can you think of a time when your prayers 'turned on you'?

How were you changed?

Is then prayer a tool used on occasion, or a lifestyle (I Thessalonians 5:17)?

# CHAPTER 7

# Churches Known More for *Where* They Are Than *Who* They Are

*. . . Building towers that become mausoleums for our own dry bones.*

—James M. Houston
*Joyful Exiles*

Over time the elaborate sanctuaries meant to glorify a higher being have become nothing more than reminders of a prior generation's attempts at relationship with God. This is a sad commentary, given the true vision for the church as captured in Paul's writings to the Corinthians: "And we all with unveiled faces, beholding the glory of the Lord Christ, are being changed into his likeness from one degree of glory to another; and this comes from the Lord who is the Spirit" (2 Cor. 3:18).

Eric Swanson, coauthor of *The Externally Focused Church* and member of the Leadership

Network, suggests the following paradigm shifts needed toward community transformation:

- From building walls to building bridges
- From measuring attendance to measuring impact
- From encouraging the saints to attend the service to equipping the saints for works of service
- From "serve us" to service
- From duplication of human services and ministries to partnering with existing services and ministries
- From fellowship to functional unity
- From condemning the city to blessing the city and praying for it
- From being a minister in a congregation to being a minister in a parish
- From anecdote and speculation to valid information
- From teacher to learner[1]

I can no longer defend any church whose only community identity is its building; nor can I support a congregation known more by where they are located than who they truly are in Christ and for the design of their campus over the impact on their community. Neither will I justify those professing Christianity yet housed in a church unwilling to suffer loss or risk real estate for the sake of others. The true church is the incarnation of Christ, always willing to participate in His suffering, always reflecting His compassion, and even willing to die (whether to themselves or to life itself) for His cause. When men refuse to die, religion wins!

Marcus Borg refers to spirituality as the "hatching of the heart." He goes on to say that we should be engaged in "whatever helps to open our hearts to the reality of the sacred. This awareness leads to an image of the Christian life very different from the one which I (Borg) grew up in. The Christian life is not about pleasing God the finger-shaker and judge. It is not about believing now or being good now for the sake of heaven later. It is about entering a relationship in the present that begins to change everything now. Spirituality is about a process: the opening of the heart to the God who is already here[2]"

May God burst the bubble of the church industry, rupturing the hearts of those who profess salvation as they ostracize unbelievers and hinder true community, while they practice rank religion in the name of Christ.

## Points of Reflection:

This most brief chapter challenges the thought of a building which houses programs merely for the benefit of its congregants. Stop a moment and list the justifications for your own church.

What is the clear mission of your church? Can both clergy and laity articulate that mission?

Is your church on mission?

If Christ were the CEO of your church, could He justify the Kingdom resources necessary for its functioning, given the similar activities of those churches nearby or adjacent to your own?

CHAPTER **8**

# Worship That Fails to Add Worth to Either the Worshiper or the Worshiped

*When tradition is thought to state the way things really are, it becomes the director and judge of our lives; we are, in effect, imprisoned by it.*
— Marcus Borg
*The God We Never Knew*

With each passing year of life, I am understanding more clearly the role of the church, the body of Christ, in the world. With that, I am becoming more disturbed by the direction that *churches* have taken the *church*. For this reason, I would like to build a case for departure from the context of church as we now know it and to explore a more balanced approach to following Christ. This approach is more holistic than the conventional church model and considers multiple sectors of life, thus better positioning the believer for true kingdom impact.

I believe the recent marketplace initiatives, such as the great gatherings of Promise Keepers, were about the kingdom pushing into the arenas of our lives beyond mere religion. The people of God are hungry for opportunities to bring Christ to where they live, beyond the campus programs of their churches. Social justice, economics, and environment, as well as religion, factor into the kingdom platform. But how we live as a community, how we govern, and how we earn and spend our currency are factors minimally addressed by many churches, outside the regular prelude to offerings, that is.

My intention is in no wise to harm the body of Christ, the true church of the Firstborn, or to diminish the obvious benefits received, both past and present, from the numerous places of worship that dot our landscape. These institutions and the universities founded under their leadership have been life sanctuaries for many in the time of storm and critical seedbeds of ingenuity in centuries past.

I am, however, seeking to communicate the possibility of an improved platform for fulfilling the Great Commission, a means more relevant than the church's current singular approach of a solo pulpit and outdated Christian education techniques, along with its limited inner city missions and foreign mission endeavors. Over time a do-gooder mentality has seized the American church, with its costly mission projects often enabling a subsistence mentality among indigenous peoples and serving more the benefit of the missionary and his or her programs than the true mission of ministry.

Agriculture, arts and industry (see Genesis 4:16–22) may be the secular substitutes for what otherwise would be the divine provision originally intended through personal intimacy and relationship with the Almighty. This alternative lifestyle, different from God's original intent for mankind's dependence on Him, may have been a grace moment for this rebellious clan of the first Adam.

The arts as we know them, unless truly inspired, represent only the dregs of the once spectacular creativity God planned for those who love Him. One has only to witness the demise of meaningful lyrics in our day, the elementary simplicity of the scripts used for TV sitcoms, and the dependence on sexual overtones to secure an audience for the media of today. Yet the mere residual of God within us is still sufficient to provide a creativity that sets apart *Homo sapiens* from all other beings.

Neither the arts nor hard work in industry or agriculture can bring to mankind what full intimacy with the Creator delivers. Mankind's purest joy is true worship. Yet that ecstasy often goes untapped by the desperate souls of lost humanity and is sadly unachievable if thought to be found only in religious attempts at reaching out to an unknown God housed in the isolation of failed franchises managed by denominational competitors. True "worthship" (sic) occurs, not when we gather together in a common place with common friends singing common songs, but rather when we journey with an uncommon God among uncommon people doing uncommon things! It is there that God brings value (worth) to our lives, and in return, we are deployed within the places of our vocation, our true calling, and thus bring worth to others. That is "worthship"!

It is only through intimacy with the Creator that His life brings true worth to our own, and that worth through grace is employed in the lives of others within our community. Unless He is reflected, in fact, glorified, by my life, I bring no true worth to Him and can add little to the lives of others. My worship, then, is merely art form, a poor substitute for what He originally desired at creation.

Learning to participate with Christ under the power and provision of the Holy Spirit in the midst of a secular society is the only true worship and the sole means of hope for transformation of the church and society. If Christ followers would only walk boldly into the economic challenges now facing our nation and the globe, we might possibly witness a moment of true spiritual transformation. My personal service in community, now for over thirty years, has provided a perspective found minimally among believers— at least, among evangelical churches. Commissions, planning boards, agency boards, and even the role of mayor are there for the taking if in wisdom we bring value to those with whom we serve.

When we truly find the Holy Place, often outside our "holy places," the place where the *I Am* dwells large in us, we discover who "*we Am*" in Him. Our gifts and anointing, our spiritual and human capital, come into full play in the marketplace, adding true worth to others and bringing true glory to the Creator.

Could it be that this financial earthquake experienced in 2009–10 will loosen the mortar, even displacing the stones that tend to hold Christ followers within their sanctuaries? In fact, this day of sudden foreclosure could be the Lord positioning His church to repossess the globe. So pray that His kingdom come, His will be done, on earth as it is in heaven!

## Points of Reflection:

How is your "worthship," your personal value to the Kingdom of God manifest during the workweek and within the marketplace?

Is your personal walk with Christ truly making a difference in your city?

Is your church known for its impact on the community (uncommon people doing uncommon things through an uncommon God)?

Cite examples of its impact, whether literal miracles similar to those in the early church, evidence of true cultural change or simply congregational representation among decision makers within the community.

## CHAPTER 9

# A Jesus Whose Name Is Often Used in Vain

*Cheap grace is the deadly enemy of the Church.
Cheap grace means grace sold on the market like
cheapjack's wares. The sacraments, the forgiveness
of sin, and the consolations of religion are thrown
away at cut prices.*

—Dietrich Bonhoeffer
*The Cost of Discipleship*

One of the great commandments found in Deuteronomy 5:11 is, "Thou shalt not take the name of the LORD thy God in vain: for the LORD will not hold him guiltless that taketh his name in vain." As a child, I was taught that using Jesus' or God's name in vain was not only something that parents punished but also something that brought a sense of impending eternal punishment, especially when used with a slang term in the presence of Sunday school teachers and other church leaders.

But let's think about this commandment in the light of a verse from the New Testament: "Having a *form* of *godliness,* but denying the power thereof: from such turn away" (2 Tim. 3:5, emphasis added). Maybe it's not children but churches that have missed the message. Is it using the name of Jesus as slang that troubles God or using the authority of the name in reckless ways that deliver little impact?

Jesus' very words reinforce the power of His spoken name: "Jesus came and spake unto them, saying, All power is given unto me in heaven and in earth" (Matt. 28:18); and, "Ye have not chosen me, but I have chosen you, and ordained you, that ye should go and bring forth fruit, and that your fruit should remain: that *whatsoever* ye shall *ask* of the Father in my *name,* he may give it you" (John 15:16, emphasis added). The Bible is clear on the authority assigned by the Father to that name.

Christians, however, often use the name of Jesus with little net change in circumstances beyond affording some sense of credence to their religious standing. We tack the name neatly onto the end of a public prayer—or at least we did prior to our loss of the right to use His name in public— and think that we have tapped into some supernatural power and made a bold stand for the Savior whose name we speak.

We are passionately drawn to verses like Acts 3:12–16:

> And when Peter saw it, he answered unto the people, Ye men of Israel, why marvel ye at this? or why look ye so earnestly on us, as though

by our own power or holiness we had made this man to walk? The God of Abraham, and of Isaac, and of Jacob, the God of our fathers, hath glorified his Son Jesus; whom ye delivered up, and denied him in the presence of Pilate, when he was determined to let him go. But ye denied the Holy One and the Just, and desired a murderer to be granted unto you; And killed the Prince of life, whom God hath raised from the dead; whereof we are witnesses. And his name through faith in his name hath made this man strong, whom ye see and know: yea, the faith which is by him hath given him this perfect soundness in the presence of you all.

These verses make great narrative to describe the power of the gospel, but in most cases they serve only as historical references aiding in some preacher's weekend revival messages. Few modern-day pastors, with the exception of the televangelists who dare offer the possibility of miracles, actually witness miracles in their sanctuaries. The use of the name of Jesus in the majority of churches in America is little more than a religious exercise.

In my vocation, I often use attorneys to draft documents for property closings. Those attorneys have certain powers that I as a realtor do not possess. They have been assigned those powers by the various bar associations by virtue of satisfactory completion of bar exams and completion of a juris doctorate at an accredited university.

Such is the case with the authority in Jesus' name and the authority to use His name that is granted to each believer. Such authority was assigned before the foundations of the earth, demonstrated by His power over death and verified through His appearance after the resurrection. Calvary was my near kinsman, my Boaz removing His sandal to redeem this displaced wanderer and the church at large (see Ruth 4). Once redeemed, repossessed by Him, I am assigned His power of attorney, the use of His name, so that at the mention of His name, all power in heaven and on earth are at my disposal. If one is not in position spiritually to use this name, or if in the use of His name little changes, that name has been used in vain.

For months prior to this writing, I began to sense a struggle within me when the name of Jesus was used by Christian friends, even by those in whom I placed great confidence. When His name was mentioned, my soul seemed to flinch. Then one day, as I sat at my computer working on something totally removed from these writings, I heard the Spirit speak: "Now you know how I feel." I pondered what He might be saying; then as God continued, I made the connection.

"Now you know how I feel when *they* [I heard someone say once that when God uses the word *they* with you, it's serious] use the name of my Son without truly desiring to be like Him." In this case, it was not so much a sense of a God angry at the people He loves, but more like a disappointed investor who has given His all to the stewards of His creation, even sending His Son into the vineyard, only to have them disrespect Him, deny His authority, and attempt to eliminate His influence from the vineyard (see Luke 20:9–13).

We have diminished the use of His name to just another religious icon, a Christian idol to be worshiped, rather than truly pursuing an intimate relationship with the God-man. Somewhere along the way, we have lost the ultimate desire to be transformed into His likeness or to know the full provision of the dynamic power of His name.

I guess I was the one who then became angry, not at the church only, but at me. I was the one who had ceased praying for the city, distracted by the prosperity that came through my Christian consulting business that later morphed into simply another brokerage firm. God had blessed my life, but the blessings of that life had seduced me in return. The house that was under construction when I began to pray was soon paid for, and then I reasoned that using my life skills in a coaching relationship with pastors and community leaders was a service to God. However, I had long ceased praying over the city and had in reality begun to serve the means by which that calling was to be delivered. Instead of praying in the power of His name, within a few years of blessing from my new coaching, consulting, and now real estate acquisition company, I found myself not only using His name in vain but teaching others how to do it as well.

I recently heard a story of an artist who worked diligently for some time on a masterpiece for the king. One day in his weariness, he caught sight of children building a snowman in the fresh snow that had fallen on the village earlier that morning. He had long felt the need for a break and so joined the children in building their work of art. Enchanted by the artist, the children encouraged him to help with their own sculpture, so he began to transform the face of the snowman from one with eyes of coal and a carrot nose to the very likeness of one of the children involved. He worked for hours as the children stood mesmerized, until he realized that his fingers were numb and could hardly move. He had over-exposed himself to the elements, and later in the night, he suffered illness, which eventually led to his death in the days following. The gifted sculptor lay lifeless, while the snowman had long since melted away. In his moment of distraction, he had wasted his phenomenal gift.

I and many others have spent our lifetimes attempting to work within temples, places of worship made by human hands, as a sincere means of honoring God. Yet I have often wondered if my moments in service to the church meant anything more than the aforementioned artist's snowman. Many of those facilities where I served now sit almost empty or struggle weekly to fund programs, most of which seldom reach the lost.

Now reflecting on that life and the concept of physical place offered to Moses in the construction of the tabernacle, I am convinced that the tabernacle was solely a metaphor for framing the reality of a day when His Spirit would occupy our bodies, the only true temple of God, and empower us in His name to do *even greater works* than the Christ. Those are the words of Christ. Neither Moses' tabernacle nor Solomon's temple was ever meant as a long-term architectural recommendation for building houses for God. They were necessary tools to communicate the fact that God desires a dwelling place—but one made without hands. We are His dwelling place.

If Jesus came to reflect the Father, and His Spirit came to indwell believers, the fruit of His Spirit should manifest within the people of the church, just as Jesus reflected the Father in His day. We should be able to say to nonbelievers, "If you have seen me, you have seen the Father"; or better yet, they should witness the Father in us without our having to tell them. The witness of the Father's love and His power was the reason sinners flocked to the Christ and the early church.

This witness, however, is sadly lacking in far too many churches today. Not only is His name used in vain, but God's children have lived under the signature of His name in ways that readily defame His name and His Word. How often, for example, do we boast of the fact that men die and go to hell, as if Jesus would condemn people who have never heard of Him, while He prospers the lives of those who should be sharing the message of redemption! God is not tame, but neither is He cruel. It is His will that *"none should perish."*

Jesus was God in the flesh, becoming the only true sacrifice required for our sins. "He paid a price He did not owe; I owed a price I could not pay," says the well-known chorus of the 80's. The God of the Old Testament died that the children of the New Testament might live. The God of the New Testament was raised from the dead so that children once forbidden access by the Old Testament might draw near Him through a righteousness that had long escaped them but was now freely given. By grace we are saved, not of works, so that none of us can boast (Eph. 2:9, paraphrased).

Again, it is not God's will that any should perish; He speaks to all, whether we speak to them or not. I believe that every person has heard Him. Yes, I believe all people have heard the voice of Jesus in their mothers' wombs, and that voice calling men back to Him is exhaustive in pursuit of each living being from birth to the grave. The church has simply been assigned the responsibility of clarifying and affirming that voice.

Some churches have assumed that no one hears the voice unless the message comes through them and often only within their facilities, almost as if God stopped speaking when His church was born. Worse yet, too many churches have not only sat still while hired professionals disavow that anyone still hears the voice of God but have also rushed to criticize anyone who assumes to have heard Him. But Jesus said and continues to say, "My children know My voice."

Listen to the words of Saint Augustine from his *Confessions*:

> Thou wert with me, but I was not with Thee.
> Things held me far from Thee,
> which, unless they were in Thee, were not at all.
> Thou called, and shouted, and burst my deafness.
> Thou flashed, shone, and scattered my blindness.
> Thou breathed odors, and I drew in breath
> and I sigh for Thee.
> I tasted, and hunger and thirst.
> Thou touchedst me, and I burned for Thy peace.[1]

Jesus came not only to speak for God but also to reveal God, to model God in man. Jesus Christ (not some common name, by the way, but actually Jesus the Christ, *the anointed one*) was fully God and fully man. Jesus, the fleshly son of Mary, was conceived of the Holy Spirit (yes, a miracle) and lived a life without sin as a result of that miracle. He was tempted in every way that any one of us might be tempted, yet unlike us, He remained without sin. He alone could justifiably pardon all mankind as God's sacrificial gift to man.

Fully man, Jesus learned just as we learn: through the things He suffered. He pursued His heavenly Father just as we must, yet He did it in full obedience. Now that same man, Jesus, sits with God and has become our bridge to righteousness, our advocate, our attorney before God. Because He lives and intercedes for us, we can be like Him; and through the power of His name, we can speak change to this globe. However, if we speak His name or invoke His authority and no change occurs, surely we have spoken His name in vain. God have mercy on professing Christ followers in America who daily speak His name in vain as they continue in lifestyles filled with the lust for things!

## Points of Reflection:

Could you relate to the story of the artist and the snowman?

What might that story have to do with the way we go about our kingdom lives as ministers of the gospel?

How are you using your life gifts to bring glory to God?

When you speak the name of Jesus Christ, what results can you offer attesting to the power you possess through that name?

What might God be speaking to you regarding the possession of power and authority given to you by Jesus the Christ?

# CHAPTER 10

# A Fractured Body

*At that time there were devout Jews from every nation living in Jerusalem. When they heard the loud noise, everyone came running, and they were bewildered to hear their own languages being spoken by the believers.*

*They were completely amazed. "How can this be?" they exclaimed. "These people are all from Galilee, and yet we hear them speaking in our own native languages! Here we are—Parthians, Medes, Elamites, people from Mesopotamia, Judea, Cappadocia, Pontus, the province of Asia, Phrygia, Pamphylia, Egypt, and the areas of Libya around Cyrene, visitors from Rome (both Jews and converts to Judaism), Cretans, and Arabs. And we all hear these people speaking in our own languages about the wonderful things God has done!" They stood there amazed and perplexed.*

*—Acts 2:5–12 NLT*

If that's not diversity, what is? The churches of America, however, are seldom known for such congregational diversity, although many different churches exist and are individually diverse from one another. We Christians don't seem to mingle well with those unlike us. We love to outreach but struggle when we have to commingle, all the while quoting Scriptures like those used by the apostle Paul: "For by one Spirit are we all baptized into one body, whether we be Jews or Gentiles, whether we be bond or free; and have been all made to drink into one Spirit" (1 Cor. 12:13).

Much of the church's inefficiency and lack of true diversity may find its root in the traditional segregation of its people into two distinct classes: clergy and laity. In light of the New Testament concept of the priesthood of all believers, and given the great need for getting the good news to all people, this caste system has always caused me great concern. In the world's cash economy, this is analogous to the haves and the have-nots.

With this mentality, two distinct roles emerge: that of either priest or provider, clergy or laity. Laity view those whose calling better fits the mold of clergy as being limited in any business or financial capacity and thus relegate them to isolated roles as evangelists and pastors. In turn, those same clergy are allocated much greater opportunity to minister within the institution than the laity to whom they minister. It seems that those laity, often less qualified as orators and whose life experiences have placed limitations on their access to more formal ministry preparation, find little attention given to their personal spiritual callings outside the bounds of the traditional service roles required for the status-quo maintenance of the institutional church programs and facilities.

It is these same laity, however, who are expected to bring a transfer of wealth from the cash economy into the kingdom, supporting the now more elite professional clergy, a growing number of whom seem to carry an expanding expectation of material abundance at the expense of that same laity. While both laity and clergy should know that God alone controls the power to get wealth and that a workman is worthy of his or her hire, both often behave in ways that breed competition and contempt rather than collaboration.

The preacher may take the position that a layman's prosperity is related more to the frequency of his tithe than to a strong work ethic and a well-honed skill set, though both are partially true. In fact, the church may hardly add value to the skill sets of the laymen even though their tithing remains timely. As a result, these people of the pew may grow up in the church with little understanding or empowerment for their own personal ministry. This dysfunctional system often crafts a higher skill set for church politics than for the personal discipleship promised by the church upon the believers' initial entry into membership, thus seeding a counterproductive and growing limitation on true ministry.

Ironically, when a leadership opportunity does present itself, laymen may seize the moment but rather than leading, may simply position themselves to negatively reinforce pastoral accountability as the conflict-laden culture sustains itself. Often elected by the congregation at large and based more on popularity and tenure than servant leadership, deacons may require the clergy to implement their particular industry's best practices, even though those same clergy have seldom been exposed to organizational management strategies in their formal training for ministry or in whatever limited secular life experiences they have acquired. If clergy resist this accountability, passive-aggressive behaviors may soon emerge among those laity to whom any degree of power has been delegated by the more trusting clergy. In many cases, a meager cash flow within the local church also compounds this dysfunction, creating a scarcity mentality, demoralizing both laity and clergy and undercapitalizing what should be the most well-managed and provided-for of all nonprofits. Eventually the pastor receives his or her "walking papers" and promptly leaves the city.

Both clergy and laity may mean well, but a counterproductive culture develops over time in which the propagation of the gospel is horribly impaired. The preacher promotes himself as possessing the sole ability for ministry to the saints, while the saints attempt to prove that they alone possess the business acumen necessary to lead the institution. So goes the story of great church battles and burnouts.

In this setting, clergy strive weekly to manufacture some meager sense of worship through liturgy or praise, ancient hymns, or contemporary songs. Some even add spiritual dance in sanctuaries where true movement of the Spirit has long been lost. Others simply wear less formal attire, sarcastically referred to as "jeans and gel." Somehow both clergy and laity have been duped into believing that service times are their only worthwhile kingdom moments, while thousands of hours of anointed marketplace ministry opportunities often go overlooked or untapped.

Interestingly enough, true marketplace impact has always been most evident among the more recent converts as they express their newfound zeal and desire to share life. It is only as the church "disciples" them, that they turn inward, "working for God" and moving deeper each week into a life surrounded by institutional service and Christian sameness. The potential for impact on the highways and hedges is gradually restricted, with their witness isolated to the aisles and classrooms of their individual facilities. Attempts at sharing Christ become more about a personal invitation to a church building than a passionate attempt to offer the gift of life that they once professed.

Meanwhile, laity stream in and out of the various churches in our communities, exhausting both tithe and talent in search of a pastor who will provide them with a fresh word from the Lord. They seek someone to acknowledge and affirm their call, to offer some understanding of that sense of eternity written in the hearts of every human.

So goes a self-defeating strategy from the kingdom of darkness that continues to stoke internal competition as a means of keeping the institutions powerless and the prophetic voice of God's church silent.

This next statement is said with all caution, yet must not be avoided if I am to stay true to the purpose of this book:

*The concept of isolated congregations within cities, as is the case both within and among the various denominations as well as in many of the nondenominational congregations that have sprung up over recent decades to combat this same problem, is at best self-defeating and at worst a deliberate containment strategy from hell assuring that Christian influence stays captive within the sanctuaries while the true voice of Christ is lost from the marketplace.*

There—as agonizing as it is, I've said it. Never again would I give thirty-five years of my life to helping sustain such a kingdom travesty. Hopefully, I have not lost my readership but rather added one more ice axe to the arsenal of reform!

## Points of Reflection:

Again, it is recommended that you pause and reflect on the emotions felt while reading the previous chapter.

What are your thoughts on the dysfunctions evident between clergy and laity in many of today's churches? How might that be remedied?

Is your church producing outcomes that model unity and glorify Christ within your city? Are those outcomes truly evident to those not attending your church? Cite examples:

# CHAPTER 11

# A Faith Seldom Manifested in the Marketplace

*Now faith is the substance of things hoped for, the evidence of things not seen.*

—Hebrews 11:1

Previous chapters suggest that my generation has maintained a profession of faith while lacking true possession of that faith or any authority on which to act. When true faith is possessed, it eventually will evidence itself by some tangible means. To paraphrase the prophet Isaiah, His Word cannot return void but will accomplish the purpose for which He intended it, wherever it is sent.

The mystical writings of the Bible were never meant simply for quotation during some religious service, far removed from real life and lost under the ceilings of ornate sanctuaries. These timeless words are about action, practice outside our sacred spaces. Had they been written only as religious literature, the writer of James would never have countered the writer of Hebrews with language like, "But wilt thou know, O vain man, that faith without works is dead?" (James 2:20).

Faith is about a courageous walk with a living Lord. True faith, like true prayer, springs out of journey, not some isolated sacred moment, though grace at times does provide those moments of reward. Those moments, which may even be ecstatic, are rightfully experienced in corporate worship among those of common faith, but they were never meant to be the sole expression of faith. By and large, the men of God selected for exposure in the New Testament were not the leaders of the synagogues, but those who created moments of faith in the streets of their cities.

True faith is a workplace phenomenon, a salt-and-light drama played out in the day-to-day life of the Christ follower. Those in true faith accept His sacrifice for sin and receive His righteousness as their own, affording the Holy Spirit full access to their lives and to the lives of those around them. Their lives become less about being churched and more about being Christ. Yes, we like Christ can become the anointed ones, the sons of God, manifesting Jesus to those who do not know Him or have not yet experienced the fullness of an intimate relationship through the work of His salvation.

This is not careless talk, but rather spiritual reality. Jesus, the son of Mary, was also the Son of God, the anointed one, the Christ. Through His sinless life and selfless sacrifice, we can know that same anointing, our lives shedding light for this globe and providing the same salt as did this Firstborn of many brethren.

Christ in us, the hope of glory, was not intended as poetry, but as the reality of the Godhead manifested bodily on this earth through the body of Christ, the church triumphant. God never intended some weak, religious, divided approach such as is now witnessed in the churches of our land, with the leadership competitive and the "follow-ship" isolated in facilities dotting almost every street corner yet bringing little or no solution to their immediate neighborhoods. These symptoms of dysfunction are, unfortunately, becoming the norm for the American church.

A faith practiced only on the Sabbath is a "faith" imprisoned to the sanctuary, sterilized by the ritualistic liturgy of churches and fit only for the dung hill. Surely Christ's brutal suffering purchased more than that for the church at large. His very prayer brought focus to the call of bringing His kingdom to this earth. His death secured and His resurrection delivered the kingdom to earth, as He had earlier prophesied to His disciples: "Verily I say unto you, there be some standing here, which shall not taste of death, till they see the Son of man coming in his kingdom" (Matt. 16:28).

Those men have died, yet they all saw Him resurrected, so surely His kingdom has already come. Our task, then, is to manifest that kingdom to others. To spend our time discussing when He will bodily return and what our role or reward might be in that new heaven and new earth can become such a distraction that we miss the mission launched by His first appearance.

Our mission is to manifest Christ through leadership within the cities of our individual callings.

My objective has long ceased to be about church planting, and my hope is that eventually those planted will be transformed as well. My last fifteen years have provided the following seven thresholds to that mission:

## The Seven Steps to Transformation

### 1. Prayer: The Catalyst for Personal Transformation

The Christian life must first involve a journey inward, a hatching of the heart; then, though at times parallel, a journey outward begins. Our journey outward as followers of Jesus advocates for the dream of God, a politic of compassion. Such is the kingdom of God on earth.

I am enough of a realist to acknowledge that we will never achieve the full kingdom of God on earth until the Christ is bodily among us, but there are approximations of what it would be like recorded in many voices in the biblical tradition. We read of justice rolling down like many waters; the lion lying down with the lamb; the earth as the pasture of God; and a time when men will beat their swords into plowshares, or "our tanks into tractors," as phrased by Reverend Joseph Echols Lowery during the presidential inauguration in January 2009. The Scriptures speak of that time when the hills will drip with honey and the mountains run with wine, when our covenant with God will be written on our hearts, and, as quoted often in our hardships, a time when there will be no more grief or sorrow and every tear will be wiped away.

These last few references are taken from the concluding chapter in John's Revelation and suggest that the dream of God takes us beyond what we now know as life on earth. However, I am convinced that the dream of God is not only for "His-story" but also for our story as well, a dream that at least in part is for the here and now. Prayer brings us to that place or, rather, brings that place to us.

Henri Nouwen, is quoted as saying: "Although we often feel a real desire to pray, we experience at the same time a strong resistance. We want to move closer to God. . . but the closer we come to him, the more intimately and urgently we experience his demand to let go of the many familiar ways in which we organize our lives. Prayer is such a radical act because it asks us to criticize our whole way of being in the world, to lay down our old selves, and to accept our new self, which is in Christ." [1]

When prayer turns in on us, compassion is birthed. No longer are we content to simply be called Christian, at least in the way my generation has come to know Christianity in America. Rather, just as was true with Christ, we also are moved with compassion, bowels of compassion. All human need becomes our own, and a new sense of "otherward" takes over our being.

Moved by this compassion, we believe deeply that no human need exists without divine provision. Yes, and even as did Christ, we find ourselves weeping over our own Jerusalem, unable to casually watch others suffer while knowing that we have life abundant. When prayer has birthed compassion in us, seldom will our contributions to others' lives be measured first against the possibility of an IRS deduction!

## 2. Compassion: The Impact of True Prayer

First John 3:17 says, "But whoso hath this world's good, and seeth his brother have need, and shutteth up his bowels of compassion from him, how dwelleth the love of God in him?" True compassion demands response, "for the love of Christ constraineth us" (2 Cor. 5:14). It requires more than small-group discussions, church committees, board approval, or any of the other moblike behaviors of today's Christianity that is afraid to stand alone and speaks boldly only within the walls of its sanctuaries or in large gatherings of protest! Could it be that Christians of this ilk are really only looking for relief from the Christ within them?

Wilbur Rees has expressed it perfectly, describing our bargaining for only a small, comfortable amount of God:

I would like to buy $3 worth of God, please.
Not enough to explode my soul or disturb my sleep,
but just enough to equal a cup of warm milk
or a snooze in the sunshine.
I don't want enough of God to make me love a black man
or pick beets with a migrant.
I want ecstasy, not transformation.
I want warmth of the womb, not a new birth.

I want a pound of the Eternal in a paper sack.
I would like to buy $3 worth of God, please.[2]

## 3. Strategic Ministry: The Response to Godlike Compassion

True compassion always brings along its sister, wisdom. Blind compassion is solely emotional; it costs the Christian little and rewards the doer more than those for whom the good is being done. Compassion birthed apart from prayer always begets do-gooders. I once read that do-gooders never eradicate the root of the problem generating their need to do good, for if they did, they would eliminate the source of ecstasy they feel as they do good. As sick and disturbing as it sounds, much of what we do as churches and individual Christians, when birthed apart from prayer, is solely for our own well-being.

Wisdom is the foundation of legacy and lays the groundwork for true compassion, transformation, and selflessness. It is not only about giving out fish but also about teaching others the secret of building their own ponds. It's about sharing life long enough so that recipients can possibly create and sustain their own resources. Food pantries and clothes closets are the easy way out, often done in convenient places close to our own campuses and with strict policies and narrow hours.

Truly strategic ministry, however, fits within a community's own vision and guards community input. It is delivered where "they" live, speaks their language, and is there when crises occur. It almost always taxes the budget, tires the volunteers, and challenges the annual business-meeting attendees.

This type of strategic ministry is seldom accomplished by the average church, parachurch, or social agency. The most successful are those driven by passionate, God-intoxicated entrepreneurs that few understand. However, these few Mother Teresa types are the best mentors to disciple true transformers and understand the eventual legacy that God will reward in the new heaven and new earth.

## 4. Discipleship: The Effect on Those with Whom and to Whom We Minister

Discipleship is not a class; it's a journey of risk. Neither Christian education nor small groups nor Sunday school can ever pay the same dividends as journeying with a mentor. I am now over a decade into this seven-step process, and the people whom I have met while in ministry to our city have changed my life, as well as having their own lives changed as a result of our interaction. The change within these servant leaders is evidenced by their consistent involvement in the challenges of our city, with the personal impact of those individuals often exceeding the impact of entire places of worship. Many have truly risked houses and lands, and some have resigned pulpits or left career paths for full marketplace service. Again, this is my reason for repenting from a quarter of a century spent "entertaining" others in local Christian education programs on segregated campuses across our land.

## 5. Revolution: The Day When the Disciples "Get It"

I am convinced of a day when true revolution will begin in our cities. Apart from any organized effort on the part of one or many churches, it will be little more than those aforementioned disciples coming together in the true wisdom and power of the Holy Spirit, utilizing in the streets of their cities what God has already cultivated in their individual hearts. When revolution comes, this movement will catch many a pastor off-guard, though good men initially called of God, they were simply unwilling to risk their careers when hungry laymen in search of true ministry first challenged them. Consequently, when the day of revolution comes, many churches will be found vacant, having served only to contain and even restrain the sons of God, as liberty finally grips the souls of this once captive priesthood of believers.

## 6. Transformation: The Church's "Aha" Moment

The institutional church will be awakened by this revolution, possibly simultaneously with a time when their facilities begin to go into default—yes, literal foreclosure. That time may be fast approaching, if not upon us now.

Propped up by well-meaning coaches and consultants, churches delay the inevitable, playing with the hopes of lay leadership through motivational hype and contemporary leadership language. Already some churches are being closed or merged by necessity, and others forestall financiers with righteous talk and spiritual shenanigans. That day is also nearing an end, as the credibility of generations past wears thin.

God is not mocked, nor will He allow the industry of church to hinder the advancement of *the* church, His body. This revolution will not be some cyclical reformation with minimal generational tweaking, a "jeans and gel" approach with high-tech video, smoke machines, and contemporary worship; but rather it will be full *repossession*—not of the sanctuaries alone, but of the temples within those sanctuaries!

## 7. Legacy: The Reformer's Reward

"And when the chief Shepherd shall appear, ye shall receive a *crown* of glory that fadeth not away" (1 Pet. 5:4, emphasis added). That's the legacy that awaits those whose compassion is birthed out of prayer; whose ministry is delivered out of a sense of personal calling, lubricated by the tears of their own weeping, strengthened by the disciples they mentor, and built upon a ministry platform in the real world. Legacy is the promise to those willing to journey, if necessary, with Christ alone. Yet be certain, that this kind of life cannot be pursued without evidence of transforming impact on the cities through which such individuals pass!

## Points of Reflection:

Are you a legacy player? Is there a spiritual progression in your life that models Christ? Define your intentional goals for personal transformation.

If so, can you actually offer names of disciples, those who are more intentional about their walk in Christ because of your leadership, your prayers, and your compassion?

If true followers of Christ are counter cultural, will your current progression in Christ lead towards spiritual revolution in your city?

What might that look like and what might it cost you?

## CHAPTER 12

# No Clear Sense
# of Prophetic Destiny

*See now that I myself am He! There is no god besides me. I put to death and I bring to life, I have wounded and I will heal, and no one can deliver out of my hand. I lift my hand to heaven and declare: As surely as I live forever, When I sharpen my flashing sword and my hand grasps it in judgment, I will take vengeance on my adversaries and repay those who hate me.*
— Deuteronomy 32:39–41

We are at a time of tremendous potential for both a transformational move of God and a technological revolution that could push our capacity as humans to a level never before comprehended, even among science-fiction writers. Our globe is perched on the precipice of disaster. Meanwhile, mankind presses forward with a boastful forecast of a point in time when machines will outwit mankind, when cheap laptops have more artificial intelligence than the natural minds that manufactured them.

To quote John Petersen from *A Vision for 2012*:

"We are entering an era that is surely going to try our souls, as we beg and scream for radically new perspectives and approaches to events and combinations of threats that humanity has never had to deal with before. At the same time, amazing, unbelievable breakthroughs in knowledge, mindsets, and capabilities will emerge just in time to be applied to the looming unpredictability that will be both strange and foreboding." [1]

Project a little further and envision a time when those machines are being manufactured and managed by a second generation of machines. Given the state of nanotechnology, human implants would then be increasingly available and become more popular and affordable. As attempts are made to improve on humanity, a day can be foreseen when implants exceed natural body mass, a time when one no longer recalls how much of himself remains human and how much machine—the ultimate evolution!

Don't lay down the book just yet, as my reason for that previous entry was to reveal where some minds are going; minds seldom reached by the message and the means of current churches. However, those same minds are busy impacting the thoughts of the children on our globe, their gifted minds and the resulting technologies fueling a rapidly expanding yet volatile economy. This same economy provides the wherewithal to spread the gospel of self-actualization and spiritual arrogance, potentially producing a generation that shakes its fist at God, while the church with its scarcity mentality barely holds its own in the world.

Where is the God of Elijah? A better question might be, where are the Elijahs of God? Many challenges face our planet, if the Lord tarries.

That phrase, *if the Lord tarries,* is a curious phrase that I have heard all my life. I was raised among dispensationalist people who believed that God designed His creation in the way that Scripture actually prophesies. And yes, I too believe that the Holy Writ both describes the process of creation and defines the boundaries of that creation to the full point of its demise.

My life was framed by Scriptures such as 2 Peter 3:2–10:

> I want you to recall the words spoken in the past by the holy prophets and the command given by our Lord and Savior through your apostles.
>
> First of all, you must understand that in the last days scoffers will come, scoffing and following their own evil desires. They will say, "Where is this 'coming' he promised? Ever since our fathers died, everything goes on as it has since the beginning of creation." But they deliberately forget that long ago by God's word the heavens existed and the earth was formed out of water and by water. By these waters also the world of that time was deluged and destroyed. By the same word the present heavens and earth are reserved for fire, being kept for the day of judgment and destruction of ungodly men.
>
> But do not forget this one thing, dear

friends: With the Lord a day is like a thousand years, and a thousand years are like a day. The Lord is not slow in keeping his promise, as some understand slowness. He is patient with you, not wanting anyone to perish, but everyone to come to repentance.

But the day of the Lord will come like a thief. The heavens will disappear with a roar; the elements will be destroyed by fire, and the earth and everything in it will be laid bare.

Many of our contemporary "brothers" scoff at this apocalyptic approach as an overly simplistic misinterpretation of the Scriptures. From their perspective, the Scriptures, though possibly inspired, reflect more the culture at that time than an inspired and relevant word for our own times. The more fundamentalist among us are assumed to have mistaken as literal what the writer of the letters meant to be figurative. I must challenge that logic and hope that any reader of this ilk will continue reading. Otherwise, the reader might consider that reluctance as symptomatic of the same narrow-mindedness previously assigned to the literalists.

The canon of Scripture was ordered by Constantine as a means of providing a government-sanctioned document for the numerous sects that would emerge within each new city conquered. It served as a constitution for his day and was an attempt to encapsulate the message of numerous manuscripts and accounts that had accumulated throughout Christendom, then spanning several continents since the death of Christ. Hundreds of manuscripts from multiple authors were examined for validity and reliability by comparing them with texts derived directly from those who had personally been with Christ, such as Luke the physician. These minimal books and letters, first only eighteen and now twenty-seven, were bound together, along with the Jewish manuscripts, to compose both an Old and a New Testament for use as a common book of order. Christianity was thus the means of bringing stability to new cities founded within the empire.

Given the fact that humans recorded the contents of the sixty-six books of the Bible across several centuries, it is indeed miraculous that such a rich story emerged. Perhaps God used Constantine's need for order as a means of capturing truth for all posterity. Unique among all books ever written, the Bible accurately foretells specific events in detail many years, even centuries, before they occurred. Approximately twenty-five hundred prophecies appear in the pages of the Bible, about two thousand of which have already been fulfilled to the letter—no errors. Since the probability for any one of these prophecies to be fulfilled by chance averages less than 1 in 10 (figured very conservatively), and since the prophecies are for the most part independent of one another, the odds for all these prophecies to be fulfilled by chance without error is less than 1 in $10^{2000}$—one with two thousand zeros written after it.[2]

A babe born in Bethlehem, which was predicted hundreds of years before His time, has been celebrated for centuries as the Messiah. Also prophesied was the rejection of that same Messiah by those to whom He was sent. Should we dare discount writings from that same script that also imply His soon return? I would ask that one reconsider the previous citation from the writings of the apostle Peter.

Some interpret 2 Thessalonians 2:3–7 to imply that Christ will catch away, or rapture, His church with little warning beyond that recorded in Scripture. This catching away of the saints could be an act of grace, since the world will continue in the absence of the stabilizing presence of the Holy Spirit.

Second Thessalonians 2:8–12 reads:

And then shall that Wicked be revealed, whom the Lord shall consume with the spirit of his mouth, and shall destroy with the brightness of his coming: Even him, whose coming is after the working of Satan with all power and signs and lying wonders, and with all deceivableness of unrighteousness in them that perish; because they received not the love of the truth, that they might be saved. And for this cause God shall send them strong delusion, that they should believe a lie: That they all might be damned who believed not the truth, but had pleasure in unrighteousness.

Many theologians interpret the writings of Daniel as offering a number of years, if not days, that must transpire as we move toward Armageddon. These numbers are reaffirmed in John's Revelation. Still others, however, see our world as having already entered a time of great tribulation, and only after Armageddon will we see Christ, they say. The logic behind this interpretation is that a time necessary for purging the church must occur, following which only the elect will be saved.

Obviously, there are many opinions within the church at large. Even if one discounts all the ancient writings, the turmoil that has now arisen in the Middle East over the world's oil reserves, the power and wealth of despots now in control of the many small developing countries, and the growing hatred for the nation of Israel should foster some validity for these thoughts. The prophecies of great armies from the east that will cross the Euphrates into Israel become more real each day as the economy of China churns anew with resources once available only to the United States. In fact, as of this writing, China is the one providing the source of debt that is keeping our own country from folding beneath global financial woes unlike any seen since the Great Depression.

Could 9/11 actually portend a time when this former bastion of belief we call America, seduced by its own wealth and now failed at both Christianity and economics, will suddenly be destroyed in one hour as leaders of our world weep in disbelief? Revelation 18:18–23 reveals such a possibility. Could the light of the gospel be snuffed out in a brief moment by some tiny rogue nation like Iran or North Korea? Could our nation, once founded on the principles of the Deity, overlook a prophetic warning for modern Babylon? Is modern Babylon our nation; and if so, could our future be some tragic irony brought on by our involvement with the geographical Babylon (Iraq), our sins as a nation actually luring us into a weakened position and seducing us into war with this ancient nation of debauchery?

Consider Luke 21:24: "And they shall fall by the edge of the sword, and shall be led away captive into all nations: and Jerusalem shall be trodden down of the Gentiles, until the times of the Gentiles be fulfilled." Christ Himself in Luke 21:32 warned that once Jerusalem was no longer under the control of Gentiles, as may have occurred in 1948, "this generation shall not pass away." Born after 1948, many Christ-following baby boomers such as this author must consider the significance of that date. Even those who choose not to believe that prophecies from the Old or the New Testament might be God-breathed certainly have to take into consideration such prophecies, given their alignment with present-day events.

Those who profess such beliefs know as well that the same testaments indicate that just before the times spoken of by the prophets, the Jews would be mysteriously attracted back to their homeland, especially those from the north. These Jews, often referred to as Russian Jews, have been silently matriculating back to Jerusalem for decades. Likewise struggling to enter and practice Judaism in their homeland, Czech Jews have in recent years created an additional immigration challenge for Jerusalem.

Impossible prior to satellite television is the prophecy found in Revelation 11:3–14 that describes the moment when two prophets will be killed in the streets of Jerusalem in plain view of the entire world. Then, after three and a half days, the world will witness the resurrection of those same two prophets as a testimony of God's power. Additionally, there will be wars and rumors of wars, famine, earthquakes, seas that die, the sun blackened from view, and a vast army that will develop to the east of Israel.

The bear from the north (thought by some theologians to be Russia), once crippled with its empire disassembled, will align again with an eastern foe. Today, that would likely be China.

Is Armageddon simply ancient folklore? Will we be able to fully protect ourselves and escape these prophecies of doom by way of some technological enlightenment, even compounding our intellect through cerebral implants such as are now being discussed in the field of bioethics?

Thomas Merton said on April 17, 1965:

Unless man turns from his idols to God, he will destroy himself, or rather this idolatry will prove itself to be his destruction. (The idolater is already self-destroyed.) The other thing: a man as a whole will not change. He will destroy himself. The Bible sees no other end to the story. But Christ has come to save from the destruction all who seek to be saved. In and through them he will recreate the world. By no means are we to interpret this to mean that enlightened ethics and polite good intentions are going to make technological society safe for man, and that a new creation will be in fact the technological paradise (plus a renewed liturgy!)[3]

God ultimately orders creation and has preserved the environment even when we fail at stewardship. He appoints and dethrones political leaders and controls the outpouring of spiritual renewal (the only true power behind religion). He alone controls the hidden truths of prophecy, securing the future of the creatures He loves against that day of destiny. He remains in the heavens, distant though ever present, sovereign yet affording us choice.

My heart sings with a sense of excitement as God unfurls His glory over this age of nanotechnology. Whether we find Him as we mine the depths of the mitochondria or the expanse of the mighty universe, God's fingerprints, God's *voice*, is there, the voice of security for our crises, the voice of love in our lostness. I personally long to see the day that mankind, once having exhausted its phenomenal ability and the God-given lust for understanding its origin, confronts the voice of God.

That day may be upon us, as atomic theory and Newtonian physics, even the quantum theory once held as absolute truth, are finding higher ground around a 1990s idea known as *string theory*. Minute particles of compressed electrical energy, once described to high-school science students of the 1980s as atoms, too small for our existing technology to magnify, have now been found to be more than vibrating particles once thought to create electromagnetic waves. It appears that they are, in fact, harmonic strings of energy that when viewed with limited magnification only appeared to be particulate. The fascinating implication is that we may be more sound than solid! In the beginning God spoke (voice, sound, harmony), and we were created. In the end, He will speak again!

This present time of economic challenge, foreclosures, and repossession could be the manifestation of a time when the true repossession that John saw in Revelation unfolds. Look at what Revelation 5:5–14 says:

And one of the elders saith unto me, Weep not: behold, the Lion of the tribe of Judah, the Root of David, hath prevailed to open the book [the deed], and to loose the seven seals thereof.

And I beheld, and, lo, in the midst of the throne and of the four beasts, and in the midst of the elders, stood a Lamb as it had been slain, having seven horns and seven eyes, which are the seven Spirits of God sent forth into all the earth. And he came and took the book [the deed] out of the right hand of him that sat upon the throne. And when he had taken the book [the deed], the four beasts and four and twenty elders fell down before the Lamb, having every one of them harps, and golden vials full of odours, which are the prayers of saints. And they sung a new song, saying, Thou art worthy to take the book [the deed], and to open the seals thereof: for thou wast slain, and hast redeemed us to God by thy blood out of every kindred, and tongue, and people, and nation; And hast made us unto our God kings and priests: and we shall reign on the earth. And I beheld, and I heard the voice of many angels round about the throne and the beasts and the elders: and the number of them was ten thousand times ten thousand, and thousands of thousands; Saying with a loud voice, Worthy is the Lamb that was slain to receive power, and riches, and wisdom, and strength, and honour, and glory, and blessing. And every creature which is in heaven, and on the earth, and under the earth, and such as are in the sea, and all that are in them, heard I saying, Blessing, and honour, and glory, and power, be unto him that sitteth upon the throne, and unto the Lamb for ever and ever. And the four beasts said, Amen. And the four and twenty elders fell down and worshipped him that liveth for ever and ever.

Could we be in the era when Jesus, our near kinsman, claims His bride and repossesses His church? In preparation of the bride, is He in fact calling His church to repentance? Could that repentance then reposition that transformed church for renewal and replenishment in this country as a final act of grace? "If my people, who are called by my name, will humble themselves and pray and seek my face and turn from their wicked ways, then will I hear from heaven and will forgive their sin and will heal their land" (2 Chron. 7:14 NIV). That is the heavenly record and personally, that is my belief.

## Points of Reflection:

Have you taken the time to personally consider the consequences of prophecies recorded in both the Old and New Testaments?

What role does prophecy play in your Christian world view?

Given current events both globally and within our nation, what should be the response of Christ followers to these ancient prophecies?

What are the implications of such prophecies in light of the scientific and technological breakthroughs of our day?

# Repent, Reposition, and Replenish

*For behold this selfsame thing, that ye sorrowed after a godly sort, what carefulness it wrought in you, yea, what clearing of yourselves, yea, what indignation, yea, what fear, yea, what vehement desire, yea, what zeal, yea, what revenge! In all things ye have approved yourselves to be clear in this matter.*

—2 Corinthians 7:11

I find it quite ironic that this final chapter just happened to be Chapter Thirteen, a law synonymous with bankruptcy. When one files bankruptcy under Chapter 13, he/she may keep property, but must earn wages or have some other source of regular income and agree to pay part of that income to creditors. One's repayment plan and budget must be approved by the courts. A trustee is appointed and will collect payments, pay creditors, and make sure one lives up to the terms of the repayment plan. Bottom line, there are penalties and limitations imposed when bankruptcy occurs, but the design is toward grace. Likewise, the Lord never places on us a burden beyond what we can bear, "but will with the temptation also make a way to escape, that ye may be able to bear it" (I Corinthians 10:13).

Just as the Federal Courts provide grace for the debtor, so is the Lord merciful toward His church. Throughout this book, I have attempted to present the practical outworking of three words God gave me in prayer late in 2008: *repent, reposition* and *replenish*. In this last chapter, I would like to elaborate on these words and offer corresponding thoughts of what churches might look like if they dared to take these words as their own.

## Personal Repentance

I first really noticed 2 Corinthians 7:11 in 1974, shortly after committing my life to Christ. Though raised in church and having had many encounters with Christ, I must have been a hard nut to crack, as I only came to true repentance at the age of twenty-five. Yet in that moment—and it seemed no longer than that—my life was refreshed and renewed in such a profound way that upon arriving at this Scripture passage some months later, I was awestruck with the language.

I had grieved for more than three years following a devastating divorce. Stubbornly resisting religious and often emotional appeals from well-meaning family and friends encouraging me to turn to Christ, I found myself wrestling through numerous relationships and using alcohol as my primary sedative. It was not until I walked into my father's home late one night and discovered him praying for me that true repentance occurred as I finally surrendered my life to Christ.

That sudden recognition of Christ's reality and a quiet sense of grace overcame all fear. The song was true: "Twas grace that taught my heart to fear, and grace my fears relieved." Christ had penetrated my heart, and by grace He had given me "beauty for ashes, the oil of joy for mourning, the garment of praise for the spirit of heaviness" (Isa. 61:3). That night I discovered a repentance that led to a great sense of cleansing, a clearing of myself, a new carefulness, awe, and a passionate desire to follow hard after Christ. I now could fully appreciate the text from 2 Corinthians 7.

Yet thirty-five years later in my life, I find a need for fresh repentance, not as much from blatant sins as from old wounds, the disappointment of missed moments, and the subtle things that creep in and put down roots of occupation in the soul. We all have sinned; and as John shared in his first epistle, if we say we have no sin, we make God a liar. Strong words! It was this need for repentance that first caught my attention that morning during my personal devotions when this book was birthed.

My first inclination after God spoke the words *repent, reposition,* and *replenish* was to move into personal repentance for my own life, excited to think that at my age I could repent in earnest and then have God reposition me for heightened kingdom impact. I was truly moved by the possibilities, especially the third promise of replenishing, which I interpreted as my physical strength and financial resources. Within a couple of weeks, doors of opportunity began to open in areas of leadership that could reposition my life in service to the community, so much so, in fact, that I became almost distracted from the continuing voice of the Lord that would eventually bring a sense of higher purpose for this word than my own personal repentance.

In the days that followed, I began to sense a broader word from the Lord, not only a call for personal repentance but also a call to the church at large. When I first began praying for my city, I was praying for "them." This time, following this word from the Lord, I was praying for me—at least initially. But the word was, in fact, for "them"— not the lost, but the church. It became increasingly painful for me to listen to the prayers offered within churches, prayers that were materialistic and prayers of bargaining for corporate wants, even prayers that others would repent. Seldom did I hear prayers of remorse and responsibility for where the churches have allowed this nation to go. It was as though we were the blind leaders of the blind!

The great commandment stresses that there are to be no other gods before Him, but do we really live this out in our day-to-day lives. Recently, as I listened during an emotional worship service to a chorus passionately exalting God above all gods, God spoke a grievous word to me. His words: "The American church has learned how to exalt me (Him) above all other gods but is unaware of any necessity and void of any intent to cast aside those other gods." We simply exalt Him above them. Our gods of materialism, racism, and capitalism are simply placed below Him as we attempt to sustain some sanctuary for our lives through corporate worship.

Repentance for America must come first in the church, a church that has taken on the nature of its fallen country, falsely prophesying what neither wealth nor democracy can deliver: *abundant life.* Abundant life does not consist of what one owns or the liberties that one may have; far more people on this globe know abundant life yet have little to eat and often live in dark cells.

Such talk, however, is foreign to the church in America, a church whose spiritual dysfunctions are as obvious as the financial symptoms of foreclosure discussed earlier in this book. God is serious about repossessing His church, a church envisioned by Him as a bride without spot or blemish. "If my people who are called by my name will humble themselves and pray and turn from their wicked ways, then . . ."

## Corporate Repentance

They lay themselves down beside every altar on garments taken in pledge, and in the house of their God they drink the wine of those who have been fined.

—Amos 2:8

Thus says the LORD of hosts, the God of Israel: You have seen all the disaster that I brought upon Jerusalem and upon all the cities of Judah. Behold, this day they are a desolation, and no one dwells in them, because of the evil that they committed, provoking me to anger, in that they went to make offerings and serve other gods that they knew not, neither they, nor you, nor your fathers. Yet I persistently sent to you all my servants the prophets, saying, 'Oh, do not do this abomination that I hate!' But they did not listen or incline their ear, to turn from their evil and make no offerings to other gods. Therefore my wrath and my anger were poured out and kindled in the cities of Judah and in the streets of Jerusalem, and they became a waste and a desolation, as at this day.

—Jeremiah 44:2–6

I thank God for the experience of personal repentance, yet as He continued to press this word into my life, I began to reflect upon what corporate repentance might look like in the church. Was the Lord calling for confession by the church at large, a turning away from congregational sins such as racism and political bias? I even thought of what might be included if we were to confess the sins of generations past: the massacres of monarchs, the Crusades masked under the sign of the cross, and the vile deeds of religious terrorists. Should we confess the sins of those early Protestant Deists who drafted our Constitution but somehow left uncertain their faith in Christ? That same leadership would later give way to rank capitalism, employing the economic engine of slavery that eventually divided the nation and its churches, even the once devout Moravians who settled my hometown. Parenthetically, not all those Moravian believers fell into sin, for some actually sold themselves to slave traders in order to deliver the message and compassion of Christ among individuals whose flesh was stacked belly to back in the dark bowels of the slave traders' ships. They deserve honor.

Could there be some subtle irony at work in our country, a land so divided by wealth and ethnicity? No longer able to force individuals to come bound to our land in order to secure our wealth, we are now spending huge amounts of money to prevent outsiders from invading our country's borders in search of our wealth. Wealthy tyrants now strangle the resources of a nation once known for its trust in God. Are these challenges somehow connected to our former sins?

What, then, would corporate repentance look like? Would it require churches to look again at inequities within their own congregations and communities? Would a body of believers set margins on prosperity, with no one in the congregation living for long at a less-than-livable wage or suffering inadequate provision? This might sound like socialism, so maybe developing a funding pool to promote small businesses and encourage entrepreneurial work would be a better means for addressing social justice.

What about those congregations that have remained racially segregated and moved out of transitioning neighborhoods as a means of retaining their racial identity? Would repentance require them to deliberately reposition themselves physically into areas of high need rather than follow the typical cycle of white-flight?

Then again, maybe repentance would require nothing more than one church walking over to the adjacent corner and partnering in such a way that eventually one of them no longer needed its facilities. Banks do it all the time. Think what would happen if two or more churches partnered together, liquidating their remaining facilities and reinvesting the net gains in joint programs. How about true team-work rather than competition among the remaining staff and pastors? Gone would be the struggle as to who is first called bishop or ultimately becomes the senior pastor. This level of repentance would surely require true transformation among both the leaders and their congregations, but it would restore cred-ibility and possibly rightfully reposition the church in America.

I believe many churches desire repentance, and some even hold occasional "holy convocations," mimicking the seasons of repentance described in the Old Testament. Of course, that may also be part of the problem, as those seasons over time may become nothing more than religious ritual, similar to how many now celebrate the Holy Week of Easter. We fast our chocolate and four-dollar coffees for Lent, but little changes in the way we do church.

Simply repenting in this fashion may serve little purpose, as explained in Isaiah 58:3–14:

> Wherefore have we fasted, say they, and thou seest not? wherefore have we afflicted our soul, and thou takest no knowledge? Behold, in the day of your fast ye find pleasure, and exact all your labours. Behold, ye fast for strife and debate, and to smite with the fist of wickedness: ye shall not fast as ye do this day, to make your voice to be heard on high. Is it such a fast that I have chosen?

a day for a man to afflict his soul? is it to bow down his head as a bulrush, and to spread sackcloth and ashes under him? wilt thou call this a fast, and an acceptable day to the LORD? Is not this the fast that I have chosen? to loose the bands of wickedness, to undo the heavy burdens, and to let the oppressed go free, and that ye break every yoke? Is it not to deal thy bread to the hungry, and that thou bring the poor that are cast out to thy house? when thou seest the naked, that thou cover him; and that thou hide not thyself from thine own flesh?

Then shall thy light break forth as the morning, and thine health shall spring forth speedily: and thy righteousness shall go before thee; the glory of the LORD shall be thy reward. Then shalt thou call, and the LORD shall answer; thou shalt cry, and he shall say, Here I am. If thou take away from the midst of thee the yoke, the putting forth of the finger, and speaking vanity; And if thou draw out thy soul to the hungry, and satisfy the afflicted soul; then shall thy light rise in obscurity, and thy darkness be as the noon day: And the LORD shall guide thee continually, and satisfy thy soul in drought, and make fat thy bones: and thou shalt be like a watered garden, and like a spring of water, whose waters fail not. And they that shall be of thee shall build the old waste places: thou shalt raise up the foundations of many generations; and thou shalt be called, The repairer of the breach, The restorer of paths to dwell in.

If thou turn away thy foot from the sabbath, from doing thy pleasure on my holy day; and call the sabbath a delight, the holy of the LORD, honourable; and shalt honour him, not doing thine own ways, nor finding thine own pleasure, nor speaking thine own words: Then shalt thou delight thyself in the LORD; and I will cause thee to ride upon the high places of the earth, and feed thee with the heritage of Jacob thy father: for the mouth of the LORD hath spoken it.

Repentance is not some religious gathering where we collectively confess our sins and then continue in them, but rather a call for a new order that may require us to abandon even the dearest of traditions that remind us of the past. Man is easily seduced by tradition, anxious to relieve himself of the pangs of change. Hebrews 11:15 addresses this: "And truly, if they had been mindful of that country from whence they came out, they might have had opportunity to have returned."

Where did we get the idea of church facilities anyway? Was it from the Old Testament tabernacle? Have we preserved the metaphor with brick and mortar and lost the message? Over time the church of Jesus Christ has become much more about real estate and the preservation of historical edifices than about securing the souls of mankind. Jesus has already addressed this once: "Woe unto you, scribes and Pharisees, hypocrites! For ye compass sea and land to make one proselyte, and when he is made, ye make him twofold more the child of hell than yourselves" (Matt. 23:15).

Recently while studying the book of Exodus, in chapter 26, verses 31–35, I read something that solidified my need for personal transformation:

Make a curtain of blue, purple and scarlet yarn and finely twisted linen, with cherubim worked into it by a skilled craftsman. Hang it with gold hooks on four posts of acacia wood overlaid with gold and standing on four silver bases. Hang the curtain from the clasps and place the ark of the Testimony behind the curtain. The curtain will separate the *Holy Place* from the *Most Holy Place*. Put the atonement cover on the ark of the Testimony in the Most Holy Place. Place the table outside the curtain on the north side of the tabernacle and put the lamp stand opposite it on the south side (NIV, emphasis added).

As I reread this prescription for the design of the temple, it was as if it were my first reading. I finally heard the message hidden by the traditions of the church as I knew them. The Most Holy Place, as theologians have acknowledged, was the place where the ark (symbolic of the body of Christ) resided alone, under the mercy seat of God. What a picture of the place provided by grace for the individual believer! This description details not a facility, but rather a friendship with God. The ark, nestled like a newly hatched chick under the warm covering of a protective mother hen, was a prescription for relationship with the Almighty through Christ.

This relationship would take on higher significance than either the showbread (symbolic of the Word of God) or the lamp stand (representative of the Holy Spirit), for both sat outside the Most Holy Place, a place reserved for the ark alone. This is not an attempt to downplay the work of the Holy Spirit or the Word of God, for the contemporary church has done sufficient damage to the significance of both. But the bottom line is, our relationship with the Almighty is more important than the text of Scriptures or the gifts of the Spirit. "But when he, the Spirit of truth, comes, he will guide you into all truth. He will not speak on his own; he will speak only what he hears, and he will tell you what is yet to come. He will bring glory to me by taking from what is mine and making it known to you. All that belongs to the Father is mine. That is why I said the Spirit will take from what is mine and make it known to you" (John 6:13–15 NIV).

Evangelicals revere the Word of God, Pentecostals focus on the gifts of the Spirit, and the more orthodox of believers are steeped in church traditions. All are sacred, providing means for communicating the opportunity for an intimate relationship with God. However, when the tools of relationship take precedent over the intimacy they were meant to foster, we have lost our way.

The tabernacle is so detailed in its description as a preparation for believers, moving them from the outer court, a point of entry and *inclusion* for all sinners, to a deeper place within His tabernacle. With each movement, a higher level of sanctification is required as the Most Holy Place is approached. However, the concept of the tabernacle was never meant to serve as a long-term building plan for some church facility.

I recall a phenomenal message delivered recently through Pastor Richard Kannwischer, a Presbyterian minister who visited our state. His message provided a rich context for Jesus' invitation to the wedding detailed in John 14:1–3. According to Pastor Richard, Jesus was sharing a story that His disciples would have readily understood, more so than those hearing that same story today.

In that day, when a daughter reached the age of thirteen or fourteen years, a father began to entertain requests for his daughter's hand in marriage. Once an acceptable suitor was named, the father informed his beloved daughter, offering her a cup (think about it), which upon drinking would signify her choice to receive (and it was a choice) her father's preferred groom. The groom was then beckoned by the father of the bride and introduced to her, after which he then returned to his own father's house in order to build an additional room suitable for his new bride-to-be. The homes of the more responsible fathers-in-law, especially those with multiple children, were multifamily places; in those fathers' houses were many rooms. This message was certainly not about multifamily housing, and neither was the tabernacle a lesson in church construction.

We live in a post-Calvary experience with God. At Calvary the curtain described in Exodus was torn in two from top to bottom the moment Jesus died (Luke 23:45). This opened the Most Holy Place to all men. The better High Priest spoken of in Hebrews entered the Most Holy Place by His own blood. No longer would mankind need a high priest to enter annually or daily into any place. In fact, we each were granted the righteousness to become high priests. The battle with righteousness was finished; it was now a gift so no man could boast nor want for it. Everything was changed at Calvary — we were repositioned in Christ.

## Corporate Repositioning

Jeremiah 30:17–21 says:

> For I will restore health unto thee, and I will heal thee of thy wounds, saith the LORD; because they called thee an Outcast, saying, This is Zion, whom no man seeketh after.

> Thus saith the LORD; Behold, I will bring again the captivity of Jacob's tents, and have mercy on his dwelling places; and the city shall be builded upon her own heap, and the palace shall remain after the manner thereof. And out of them shall proceed thanksgiving and the voice of them that make merry: and I will multiply them, and they shall not be few; I will also glorify them, and they shall not be small. Their children also shall be as aforetime, and their congregation shall be established before me, and I will punish all that oppress them. And their nobles shall be of themselves, and their governor shall proceed from the midst of them.

The church was repositioned in Christ; the task now is to be repositioned in America. That does not mean having evangelicals on the Supreme Court or having any particular party in the executive or legislative branches. Repositioning has more to do with credibility and community. The people of God must again begin to demonstrate the love of God, the wisdom of God, and the justice of God.

If that happened, gone would be the shenanigans of the prosperity message, the economic disparity within individual congregations, and, in fact, gone would be many of those congregations. Churches would reflect their communities, not solely the ethnicity of their tradition or the narrow doctrines of cultural comfort. When the name of Jesus was used outside of worship, powerful change would occur because the church would now understand the authority given that name. With that authority would also come righteous solutions to real-time challenges in the marketplace. No longer would Christianity be seen as merely a failed religion that functioned only within religious facilities on isolated campuses.

The vision for faith-based programs as beacons of light set on a hill would be realized as something more than well-meaning nonprofits where the well-to-do, do good. Values that reflect righteousness would again be employed in the workplace, both by CEOs and employees. Capitalism as a concept for free enterprise could also be at work, but with justice administered in a way that assured "all things common" when it came to the needs of others, yet remained far short of a liberal socialism that coddles those who will not work.

Can there be an economy this righteous? The prophet Micah thought so: "He has shown thee O man what is good, to do justice, to love mercy and to walk humbly with thy God" (Mic. 6:8).

## Corporate Replenishing

Jesus said, "I tell you the truth, at the renewal of all things, when the Son of Man sits on his glorious throne, you who have followed me will also sit on twelve thrones, judging the twelve tribes of Israel. And everyone who has left houses or brothers or sisters or father or mother or children or fields for my sake will receive a hundred times as much and will inherit eternal life. But many who are first will be last, and many who are last will be first" (Matt. 19:28–30 NIV).

God knows this next generation needs a word of hope offering something beyond Armageddon. What they need is truth, but not in word only; the church must begin to deliver in deed. May God help my generation to leave a legacy that, in fact, shared truth, even if to our peril; and if truth is Armageddon, then we should not hide it, but boldly share the reality of the life that awaits the believer once this earth is no more.

Revelation 21:1–5 speaks clearly of this life:

I saw Heaven and earth new-created. Gone the first Heaven, gone the first earth, gone the sea.

I saw Holy Jerusalem, new-created, descending resplendent out of Heaven, as ready for God as a bride for her husband.

I heard a voice thunder from the Throne: "Look! Look! God has moved into the neighborhood, making his home with men and women! They're his people, he's their God. He'll wipe every tear from their eyes. Death is gone for good—tears gone, crying gone, pain gone—all the first order of things gone" (MSG).

If we are unsure about the future, we should seek the Lord until we have a sense of our prophetic destiny, rather than dividing into camps. We do have the promise recorded in John's gospel that the Holy Spirit will take what is Christ's and show it to us.

"The first order of things gone"—Is John attempting to describe a heavenly thing that is forthcoming or something God will do on this earth when the church is repositioned? I suspect both, as that best reflects a God of second chances.

It seems that in these final paragraphs I find myself vacillating between a need to forewarn a generation of what could be ahead of our nation, the only message of the church in which I was raised, and a need to speak something of hope into the lives of those coming behind me. Does God do "both and" versus "either or"? Does prophecy truly forecast the absolute reality of our future or the results of ill choices made about our future? Do our choices push forward a day when all these things will occur? I seem to have nothing but questions at this point.

If there is hope, everything must change; everything must be laid on the altar, including our traditions, our real estate, our politics, and even our petty doctrines. Are we willing to take this risk for the sake of the greatest nation on earth? This cannot be just another call for reformation for the sake of attracting and holding a new generation within the real estate of our churches. This is war, the breaking up of fallow ground. "If my people, who are called by my name"—not the sinner—"then will I heal their land." A *replenishing* and renewal is possible, and the church can be *repositioned,* if the church will come to *repentance.*

## Points of Reflection:

Take a moment for confession on behalf of your life and the life of your church.
Why not list those confessions for accountability's sake?

Envision how true corporate repentance might change your church and how that would manifest itself in your own community?

What are you willing to do in order to facilitate change both within your own life, your church life and the 'body life' among churches in your community?

# Epilogue

# A Personal Call to Revolution

W hen in the course of human events, it becomes necessary for one people to dissolve the religious bands of denomination which have divided brother from brother, and to assume among the powers of the kingdom, the separate and equal station to which the laws of God entitle them, a decent respect to the opinions of mankind requires that they should declare the causes which impel them to the separation.

We hold these truths to be self-evident: that all men through Christ are now one priesthood, and that they are endowed by their Creator with certain unalienable rights; that among these are life, liberty, and the pursuit of personal calling. That to secure these rights, churches were in good faith instituted among men, deriving their just powers from the consent of the churched, each being led by a common Spirit and an uncommon baptism; however, when any form of governance, be it spiritual or political, becomes destructive of these ends, it is the right and the responsibility of the people to alter or to abolish it, and to institute new practices, laying its foundation on such principles, and organizing its powers in such form, as to best assure both personal destiny and kingdom mission as described by the Word of God.

Prudence, indeed, will dictate that spiritual practices long established should not be changed for light and transient causes; and accordingly all experience hath shown that mankind are more disposed to suffer, while evils are sufferable, than to right themselves by abolishing the forms to which they are accustomed.

But when a long train of abuses and usurpations, pursuing invariably the same object, evinces a design to reduce them under absolute despotism to the degree that the nation no longer is affected by the presence of such religious institutions, it is their right, it is their duty, to throw off such practices, and to provide new constructs for their future spirituality and that of their children.

And for the support of this declaration, with a firm reliance on the protection of divine providence, we mutually pledge to each other our lives, our fortunes, and our sacred honor.

—John Bost
*A spiritual modification of the initial chapters of the Declaration of Independence*

Your reflections, reactions,
applications and their results
would be of great value to this author.
Please communicate by email via
masterCounsel@triad.rr.com.

# Notes

Epigraph for book: Oscar Plook, 1904 quote: *Joyful Exiles,* James M. Houston, 2006, 25–26.

**Preface:** Jill Carattini, "Seismographs of the Soul." A Slice of Infinity, No. 1424, originally printed May 23, 2007 (www.rzim.org <http://www.rzim. org/> ). Used with permission of Ravi Zacharias International Ministries.

## Chapter 1: The Psychology and Symptoms of Foreclosure

Quote: *http://www.realtytrac.com*

## Chapter 2: Symptoms in the Sanctuary

Tom Ehrlich, http://www.morningwalkmedia.com.

Thomas Merton, *A Year with Thomas Merton,* Harper: San Francisco, 2004; January 25, 1962.

Jill Carattini, "The Shelf Life of Wisdom," A Slice of Infinity, No. 1859, originally printed February 18, 2009 (www.rzim.org <http:// www.rzim.org/> ). Used with permission of Ravi Zacharias International.

## Chapter 3: Prophets of Prosperity

Thomas Merton, *A Year with Thomas Merton*, Harper: San Francisco, 2004. May 1965, v. 239–40.

## Chapter 4: A God That Is Tame

C. S. Lewis, The Lion, The Witch and the Wardrobe, illustrated by Pauline Baynes.

## Chapter 6: Prayer, a Mere Religious Exercise

*The Transformed Friendship,* James Houston, Lion Publishing, 1989.

## Chapter 7: Churches Known More for *Where* They Are Than *Who* They Are

James M. Houston, *Joyful Exiles,* Intervarsity Press, 2006.

Eric Swanson, coauthor of *The Externally Focused Church* (Loveland, CO: Group Publishing 2004), Leadership Network.

Marcus Borg, *The God We Never Knew,* Harper: SanFrancisco, *1997,* p.128.

## Chapter 9: His Name Used in Vain

James M. Houston, *Joyful Exiles,* Intervarsity Press, 2006, p.102.

Augustine, *Confessiones* (*Confessions*), 10.27.38, the classic English translation is that of E. B. Pusey.

## Chapter 11: A Faith Seldom Manifested in the Marketplace

Henri Nouwen, http://paxetbonum.blogspot.com/2007/06/priest-as-shepherd-and-doctor-of-souls.html

Wilbur Rees, "$3 Worth of God." *When I Relax I Feel Guilty* by Time Hansel (Elgin, IL, David C. Cooke Publishing Co., 1979) p. 49.

## Chapter 12: No Clear Sense of Prophetic Destiny

John L. Petersen, *A Vision for 2012* by John L. Petersen, Fulcrum Publishing: Golden, Colorado, 2008.

Hugh Ross, Ph.D., http://www.reasons org/resources/apologetics/prophecy.shtml.

Thomas Merton, *A Year with Thomas Merton*, Edited by Jonathan Montaldo,
Harper: SanFrancisco, 2004, p.109.

CPSIA information can be obtained
at www.ICGtesting.com
Printed in the USA
BVHW071418120620
581230BV00004B/139

9 781615 790814